God's Magnificent Goodness

VOLUME ONE: VICTORIOUS CHRISTIAN LIVING

D1715125

God's Magnificent Goodness

VOLUME ONE: VICTORIOUS CHRISTIAN LIVING

Greg Backes

The Solution Publishing House
NAPERVILLE, IL

Scripture quotations are taken from the Authorized King James Version of the Bible. Other versions used are marked accordingly.
Brackets [ ] in a scripture verse indicate words added for clarity by the author.

Other books (available on Amazon Kindle):
Blessed Assurance – The Truth about Speaking in Tongues
Baptism – A Biblical Perspective
Higher Powers – Discover Their True Identity

Booklets:
The Solution
Complete in Christ
You Are Righteous Now

Greg Backes
The Solution
P.O. Box 9002
Naperville, IL 60567

www.TheSolutionRadioShow.com
info@TheSolutionRadioShow.com

Book Layout ©2021 BookDesignTemplates.com
Cover Photo – Adobe Stock #279342840

God's Magnificent Goodness / Greg Backes — 1st edition
Publication Date: March 2021
Printed by: InstantPublisher.com in the United States of America
ISBN 978-0-578-24643-7

DEDICATION

To all those that preach
and teach God's Word

To whom God would make known what is the riches
of the glory of this mystery among the Gentiles;
which is Christ in you, the hope of glory:

Whom we preach, warning every man,
and teaching every man in all wisdom;
that we may present every man perfect in Christ Jesus:

Whereunto I also labour,
striving according to his working,
which worketh in me mightily.

— Colossians 1:27-29

A NOTE FROM THE AUTHOR

Above all I am thankful to our Heavenly Father and our Lord Jesus Christ. Their love for each of us knows no bounds. Without the gift of eternal life and an understanding of the Bible, life would be meaningless. Each of us has a purpose, a future prepared before the foundation of the world by God. I am thankful for the grace and mercy God has given me.

I am also thankful to those who have taught me God's Word over the past forty plus years. They are too numerous to mention but God knows their identity and their reward at the Return of our Lord will be abundant.

My prayer is that this book will help to lead you in living a more victorious life in Christ. This is the first volume of several to follow. Each of the fourteen chapters contained in this book is a teaching from *The Solution Radio Show*.

At the time of this publication there are a total of 100 shows. There were 64 one-hour broadcasts of *The Solution Radio Show* on WBIG 1280 AM, Aurora, IL. There were 24 half-hour broadcasts on WYLL 1160 AM, Chicago, IL. and 11 half-hour broadcasts on WDZY 1290 AM, Richmond, VA and on KLNG 1560 AM Omaha, NE.

Each of the programs contained a teaching. Many of the programs also contained an interview with Christians from various backgrounds and accomplishments and some programs included Christian music.

All of the shows may be listened to in their entirety at www.TheSolutionRadioShow.com.

This book may be used to facilitate personal study of various topics and in a small group setting. Each chapter includes discussion questions to help establish God's Word in the heart of the reader.

God bless you in the mighty name of our Returning Lord, Jesus Christ!
You are God's Very Best!

Greg Backes
March 2021

ACKNOWLEDGEMENTS

Thank you to all that have listened to *The Solution Radio Show*. Thank you for your prayers, feedback, and financial support.

Thank you to Dannie Bova for editing the manuscript. Thank you to Jenn Lattimore for transcribing many of the teachings.

Contents

CHAPTER 1

God's Magnificent Goodness

The book of Ephesians is the pinnacle, the height, of what God has done for His people. Ephesians makes known the great heart of love of our Heavenly Father. It is in the book of Ephesians that we see the grace and mercy of God on full display.

Ephesians 1:1, 2

¹ Paul, an apostle of Jesus Christ by the will of God, to the saints which are at Ephesus, and to the faithful in Christ Jesus:

² Grace be to you, and peace, from God our Father, and from the Lord Jesus Christ.

It says, "Grace be to you." God's favor and God's peace to you. It does not say judgment and condemnation; it does not say the wrath of God. It says grace be to you and peace from God our Father and from the Lord Jesus Christ.

Ephesians 1:3

Blessed be the God and Father of our Lord Jesus Christ, who hath blessed us with all spiritual blessings in heavenly places in Christ:

God has blessed you with all spiritual blessings. These blessings are in heavenly places in Christ. Some of those blessings are listed here in chapter one of Ephesians.

Ephesians 1:4

According as he hath chosen us in him before the foundation of the world, that we should be holy and without blame before him in love:

God sees you as holy and without blame before him in love. God sees you that way because of what Jesus Christ has accomplished for you.

Ephesians 1:5, 6

⁵ Having predestinated us unto the adoption of children by Jesus Christ to himself, according to the good pleasure of his will,

⁶ To the praise of the glory of his grace, wherein he hath made us accepted in the beloved.

You are accepted in the beloved! I can remember growing up how badly I wanted to be accepted with the in-crowd and fit into the right group. Well, it says here that according to God, we are accepted in the beloved. There is no better group than that! You are part of the body of Christ, a part of God's family.

The word "accepted" in verse six in the Greek is very interesting. It is only used one other place in the New Testament, and that is in Luke1:28.

Luke 1:28

And the angel came in unto her, and said, Hail, thou that art highly favoured, the Lord is with thee: blessed art thou among women.

The angel told Mary that she was highly favored. Those two words, "highly favored", are the same word in the Greek as the word "accepted" in Ephesians 1:6. Mary was highly favored of God. She carried the Christ child. Mary was Jesus' mom. Do you think God took care of Mary? Sure He did. God takes care of you. You too are accepted. You too are greatly favored in the beloved; you are highly favored of God because you have Christ in you - the hope of glory!

Ephesians 1:7

In whom we have redemption through his blood, the forgiveness of sins, according to the riches of his grace;

You have redemption through the blood of Jesus Christ. You have forgiveness of sin. You have remission of the sin nature that was handed down by Adam. This redemption and forgiveness is according to the riches of God's grace! It is not according to what you have or have not done. It is according to what God has done for you through Jesus Christ.

Ephesians 1:8-10

[8] Wherein he hath abounded toward us in all wisdom and prudence;

[9] Having made known unto us the mystery of his will, according to his good pleasure which he hath purposed in himself:

[10] That in the dispensation of the fulness of times he might gather together in one all things in Christ, both which are in heaven, and which are on earth; even in him:

In the administration of the fullness of times, God is going to gather everything together in Christ. It is still future. The fullness of times will be at the return of Jesus Christ, then the fullness of times will begin. That day is going to happen. It could happen before you finish reading this sentence. It might happen before this year is over, or it may not be for another thousand years. However, Jesus Christ is coming back, and in the fullness of times when he returns, God is going to gather together everything in him.

Ephesians 1:11

In whom also we have obtained an inheritance, being predestinated according to the purpose of him who worketh all things after the counsel of his own will:

You have an inheritance in Christ having been predestinated, or chosen in advance, according to the purpose of God who works all things after the counsel of His own will. God knew you would believe His Word regarding the Lord Jesus Christ.

God could predestinate you unto the purpose of His will because of His foreknowledge.

Ephesians 1:12

That we should be to the praise of his glory, who first trusted in Christ.

The purpose behind God having predestinated you is that you should be to the praise of His glory! You trusted in Christ. You are to the praise of His glory.

Ephesians 1:13, 14

[13] In whom ye also trusted, after that ye heard the word of truth, the gospel of your salvation: in whom also after that ye believed, ye were sealed with that holy Spirit of promise,

[14] Which is the earnest of our inheritance until the redemption of the purchased possession, unto the praise of his glory.

What is the word of truth, the gospel of your salvation that you heard? You heard that God raised Jesus Christ from the dead, and you confessed him as Lord, as it says in Romans 10:9, 10. That is what we are to believe. That is the gospel of your salvation and your wholeness. You are sealed with that holy spirit of promise.

The holy spirit you have received in the new birth is the earnest of verse 14. It is the down payment of your inheritance until the redemption of the purchased possession onto the praise of His glory. You are God's purchased possession.

At the return of Jesus Christ, you will see the greatness of your inheritance which will last throughout all eternity. God has amazingly tremendous things in store for you!

Ephesians 1:15, 16

[15] Wherefore I also, after I heard of your faith in the Lord Jesus, and love unto all the saints,

[16] Cease not to give thanks for you, making mention of you in my prayers;

Paul gave thanks to God for God's people. He prayed for God's people. In verses 17 through 23 we see what Paul prayed.

This is a prayer that you can pray for yourself. This is a prayer that you can pray for your family, for your brothers and sisters in Christ, for your church. This is God's will. This is a prayer that not only can you pray, but you can know that your Heavenly Father hears you when you pray. You can expect God to answer this prayer because this prayer is His will.

Ephesians 1:17, 18

[17] That the God of our Lord Jesus Christ, the Father of glory, may give unto you the spirit of wisdom and revelation in the knowledge of him:

[18] The eyes of your understanding being enlightened; that ye may know what is the hope of his calling, and

what the riches of the glory of his inheritance in the
saints,

God has given you spiritual wisdom and understanding. In
verse 18, it states, "that ye may know…" There are three
truths listed that God desires for you to know. Three things
that you can pray that the eyes of your heart be enlightened.

Number one, what is the hope of His calling? God wants you
to know what is the hope of the calling to which he has called
you. The greatness of His calling is eternal life, which will
begin in all its magnificence at the return of Jesus Christ.
However, it is not only at our Lord's return; the greatness of
that calling is right now today, walking with our Heavenly
Father, operating the manifestations of holy spirit, healing
people, casting out devil spirits, speaking in tongues,
interpreting tongues, operating a word of prophecy. That is
part of the hope of His calling – to be able to walk in the
fullness of what God has made available to you through the
accomplished work of Jesus Christ.

Secondly, what are the riches of the glory of God's
inheritance in the saints? God wants you to know what the
riches of the glory of His inheritance is in you! You are one
of the saints referred to here. You are what God gets out of
this deal. He is pleased with you. Remember you are accepted
in the beloved. You are God's inheritance!

Ephesians 1:19

And what is the exceeding greatness of his power to
us-ward who believe, according to the working of his
mighty power,

Third, your Heavenly Father wants you to know the
greatness, the exceeding greatness, of the power that is
available for you to operate in this world today. God gives the
standard for that power in the following verses twenty
through twenty-three.

Ephesians 1:20-23

[20] Which he wrought [energized] in Christ, when he
raised him from the dead, and set him at his own
right hand in the heavenly places,

[21] Far above all principality, and power, and might,
and dominion, and every name that is named, not
only in this world, but also in that which is to come:

[22] And hath put all things under his feet, and gave him
to be the head over all things to the church,

[23] Which is his body, the fulness of him that filleth all
in all.

Wow! The power available to you is according to the working
of God's mighty power which He energized in Christ when
he raised him from the dead. Not only did God raise Jesus
Christ from the dead; He also set him at His own right hand
in the heavenly places far above all principality and power and
might and dominion. He gave Jesus Christ a name that is

above every name, not only in this world but also in that which is to come! God has put all things under his feet and gave him to be the head over all things to the church, which is his body. The fullness of God then fills, all in all, all the way out to including you!

Jesus Christ - the name that is above every name. You have the authority and the right to use that name.

That is the standard of the power that is available to the church today. It is the power that raised Jesus Christ from the dead. How much power does it take to raise someone from the dead? Jesus Christ was in the earth for three days and three nights. On the third day, God raised him from the dead. What kind of power does it take to raise someone from the dead? It takes a tremendous amount of power! That is the standard of the power that is available to you today because of what God has done for you, through you and in you. You have His holy spirit living inside of you!

Not only was Jesus Christ raised from the dead, he also ascended into heaven at God's right hand. What type of power does it take to lift someone off the earth, through the atmosphere, past the moon, the sun, the solar system, the universe, all the way through the heavens to God's right hand? It takes an amazing amount of power! That is the standard of the power that is available to you, as God's child, today!

God also gave Jesus Christ a name that is above every name. The name of Jesus Christ is so mighty and powerful! You have the authority and the right to use that name for blessing and deliverance.

In verse 22, it states that God put all things under Jesus Christ's feet, and He gave him to be the head over all things to the church. You are the church. You are part of the body of Christ. Jesus Christ is the head of that body. It states that "all things are under his feet." Well, in the body, even if you were the little toe in that body, all things are under you because you have Christ in you, the hope of glory! You have the authority to use the name of Jesus Christ!

In verse 23, it states that the body of Christ is the fullness of Him [God] that fills all in all.

As you look to God and His Word, you can begin to see the greatness of His love for you. Here in Ephesians chapter one, we have seen the great love that our Father has for His children. He wants you to know the greatness of the calling that He has called you to. He wants us to know the inheritance that He has in you, and He wants you to know the power that you may utilize. All of it – the love, the calling, and the power – is because of the accomplished work of our Lord and savior Jesus Christ!

Ephesians 2:1-3

[1] And you hath he quickened, who were dead in trespasses and sins;

[2] Wherein in time past ye walked according to the course of this world, according to the prince of the power of the air, the spirit that now worketh in the children of disobedience:

[3] Among whom also we all had our conversation in times past in the lusts of our flesh, fulfilling the desires of the flesh and of the mind; and were by nature the children of wrath, even as others.

At one time in the past, we were dead in our trespasses and sins. We previously walked according to the ways of this world. We were at one time directed by the spirit that works in those who are disobedient to God, fulfilling the desires of the flesh and of the mind.

Ephesians 2:4, 5

[4] But God, who is rich in mercy, for his great love wherewith he loved us,

[5] Even when we were dead in sins, hath quickened us together with Christ, (by grace ye are saved;)

Verse four is a huge contrast to verses one through three. God, is rich in mercy because of the great love He has for us! God has an abundance of loving kindness, and He is overflowing in His mercy toward His children.

Even when we were dead in sins, He made us alive together with Christ! It is by His unearned favor, His grace, that we have been saved! Not a one of us could save ourselves of our own ability. God stepped into our lives through His son, our Lord Jesus Christ!

Ephesians 2:6, 7

⁶ And hath raised us up together, and made us sit together in heavenly places in Christ Jesus:

⁷ That in the ages to come he might shew the exceeding riches of his grace in his kindness toward us through Christ Jesus.

He not only gave you life, He also raised you up with Christ Jesus and placed you at His own right hand to sit together with Christ Jesus! What a calling! What a destination you have – seated at God's right hand with His magnificent son, our Lord and savior!

Ephesians 2:8, 9

⁸ For by grace are ye saved through faith; and that not of yourselves: it is the gift of God:

⁹ Not of works, lest any man should boast.

It is all by God's grace. Not one of us by our good works could have earned eternal salvation – a salvation so complete that we are seated at our Heavenly Father's right hand to the praise of His glory forever! Our only boasting is in God and His magnificent goodness.

Ephesians 2:10

For we are his workmanship, created in Christ Jesus unto good works, which God hath before ordained that we should walk in them.

You are God's workmanship, and He has prepared good works for you to walk in. It is after you become born again of God's spirit, having accepted Jesus Christ as your Lord and believing that God raised him from the dead (Romans 10:9, 10), that your good works begin to matter.

Now that you have the spirit of God, your Father works within you.

Philippians 2:13

For it is God which worketh in you both to will and to do of his good pleasure.

What is it that God works within you? He works within you the good works of Ephesians 2:10. The works which He before prepared for you to do.

Wow! What a life! We have so very much to be thankful for. Our Heavenly Father is so incredibly good to each of us!

Jesus was always looking to serve his Father. He simply did what the Father showed him, he spoke what the Father spoke. You have the privilege of walking and living as Jesus Christ.

If nothing else today, know that God loves you, and that He extends toward you grace and peace - not judgment, not condemnation, not wrath. Grace and peace to you from God our Father and from the Lord Jesus Christ.

God's magnificent goodness has been showered upon you!

Discussion Questions

1. What are some of the spiritual blessings that God has blessed you with?

2. How does God see you? List scripture verses.

3. What does the prayer in Ephesians 1:16-23 tell you to pray for?

4. What is the standard of the power that is available to you today? Take a minute to dwell on the greatness of that power and to thank the Father. How might you utilize that power in your life?

5. In Ephesians chapter two it states that you are saved by grace and not of works. How has God's grace touched your life?

CHAPTER 2

The Urgency of Our Times

Today is the greatest day in the history of mankind to be alive! Why is it the greatest day to be alive? Because this timeframe, this day we are living in, is the Age of God's Abundant Grace! It is a day the prophets of old desired to see, but it was kept secret in God until it was first revealed to the Apostle Paul.

Ephesians 3:3-6

³ How that by revelation he [God] made known unto me the mystery; (as I wrote afore in few words,

⁴ Whereby, when ye read, ye may understand my knowledge in the mystery of Christ)

⁵ Which in other ages was not made known unto the sons of men, as it is now revealed unto his holy apostles and prophets by the Spirit;

⁶ That the Gentiles should be fellowheirs, and of the same body, and partakers of his promise in Christ by the gospel:

Verse six is the mystery made known to Paul. It had been hidden in all the ages, through all prior generations. God revealed to Paul that the Gentiles should be fellow heirs and of the same body. The greatness of the redemption, which became available through the life, death, and resurrection of the Lord Jesus Christ, was now open to all who would believe.

Ephesians 3:9-11

[9] And to make all men see, what is the fellowship [administration] of the mystery, which from the beginning of the world hath been hid in God, who created all things by Jesus Christ:

[10] To the intent that now unto the principalities and powers in heavenly places might be known by the church the manifold wisdom of God,

[11] According to the eternal purpose which he [God] purposed in Christ Jesus our Lord:

This day, the age of grace, the administration of which you and I live in today, is the greatest time in the history of mankind.

How BIG is this Grace? How MAGNIFICENT is this Age within which we live?

I Corinthians 2:4-8

4 And my [the Apostle Paul] speech and my preaching was not with enticing words of man's

wisdom, but in demonstration of the Spirit and of power:

5 That your faith [believing] should not stand in the wisdom of men, but in the power of God.

6 Howbeit we speak wisdom among them that are perfect [mature]: yet not the wisdom of this world, nor of the princes of this world, that come to nought:

7 But we speak the wisdom of God in a [regarding the] mystery, even the hidden wisdom, which God ordained before the world unto our glory:

Here is the key verse.

8 Which none [NONE!] of the princes of this world knew: for had they known it, they would not have crucified the Lord of glory.

That is just remarkable! It is so incredible, so awesome! It is so believable because it is God's Word. Had the devil known that you would be who you are today in this age of Grace, that you could receive God's spirit, that you could have Christ in you, the hope of glory, the devil never would have crucified the Lord Jesus Christ!

If Jesus Christ had not been crucified you might hear today on the evening news, "Jesus was in Bethlehem, Pennsylvania today, there were 18 raised from the dead and 14 received their sight. There were many other signs, miracles and wonders. It is reported he will be in Zion, Illinois tomorrow."

That could have been the newscast.

The devil knows how valuable you are to the Father. Had he known what you have today, he would not have crucified the Lord Jesus Christ. God knows how valuable you are because He gave His only begotten son for you.

In Colossians, we see the riches of the glory of this mystery.

Colossians 1:27

> To whom God would make known what is the riches of the glory of this mystery among the Gentiles; which is Christ in you, the hope of glory:

It is Christ in you, the hope of glory! What an awesome privilege to be alive!

God, since the fall of Adam and Eve in the garden, desired to reestablish a relationship with His creation – mankind. The reestablishment of that relationship became available through the life, death, and resurrection of the Lord Jesus Christ. On the day of Pentecost, God could once again place His spirit within men, women, and children. He could be a Father to His prized creation – mankind.

In the Gospel of Luke, we see Jesus Christ being tempted at the start of his public ministry.

Luke 4:5-8

> [5] And the devil, taking him [Jesus Christ] up into an high mountain, shewed unto him all the kingdoms of the world in a moment of time.

⁶ And the devil said unto him, All this power will I give thee, and the glory of them: for that is delivered unto me; and to whomsoever I will I give it.

⁷ If thou therefore wilt worship me, all shall be thine.

⁸ And Jesus answered and said unto him, Get thee behind me, Satan: for it is written, Thou shalt worship the Lord thy God, and him only shalt thou serve.

Satan offered to Jesus Christ the power and the glory of all the kingdoms of this world. He could offer it because it was his to give. The fall of Adam in the Garden of Eden was an act of treason. Adam handed over his rulership of this world to God's arch enemy, the devil.

Much like Satan's temptation in the Gospel of Luke, the things of this world are by and large, designed to keep people from knowing the one true God's love, His goodness, His mercy, and His grace.

Since the fall of Adam, man has largely been deceived by the god of this world – the devil.

II Corinthians 4:3-5

³ But if our gospel be hid, it is hid to them that are lost:

⁴ In whom the god of this world hath blinded the minds of them which believe not, lest the light of the glorious gospel of Christ, who is the image of God, should shine unto them.

> ⁵ For we preach not ourselves, but Christ Jesus the
> Lord; and ourselves your servants for Jesus' sake.

The gospel is hidden to them that are lost. The god of this
world has blinded people's eyes. It is the gospel of Jesus
Christ, it is the love of God, it is the Word of God that will
open people's eyes.

If you ask most people today what they think of God, many
will say that He is just waiting to pass judgment and
condemnation or that they do not believe in Him at all
because they have been so beat up by the lies promulgated
about Him. Even many well-intentioned religious people
misrepresent our Heavenly Father by attributing to Him the
works of the devil, such as earthquakes, violent storms,
sickness, disease and death. They state how it is God's
judgment upon unrepentant people. Hebrews 2:14 and 15
state that the devil is the author of death. The devil is the one
who puts people in bondage.

Hebrews 2:14, 15

> ¹⁴ Forasmuch then as the children are partakers of
> flesh and blood, he also himself likewise took part of
> the same; that through death he might destroy him
> that had the power of death, that is, the devil;
>
> ¹⁵ And deliver them who through fear of death were
> all their lifetime subject to bondage.

In I John 3:8 it states, "For this purpose the Son of God was
manifested, that he might destroy the works of the devil."

Jesus Christ healed people. Jesus Christ raised people from the dead. He helped people wherever he went.

There is a day coming when God will judge the world, and it is described throughout the book of Revelation. We are not yet living in the times described in the book of Revelation.

There is one great, notable event that MUST and WILL take place first. That event is the return of Jesus Christ!

I Thessalonians 4:13-18

[13] But I would not have you to be ignorant, brethren, concerning them which are asleep, that ye sorrow not, even as others which have no hope.

If God does not want us to be ignorant, He must want us to know. He does not want us to sorrow as those who have no hope.

[14] For if we believe that Jesus died and rose again, even so them also which sleep [those that have died] in Jesus will God bring with him.

[15] For this we say unto you by the word of the Lord, that we which are alive and remain unto the coming of the Lord shall not prevent [precede] them which are asleep.

Some of God's children will be alive when the Lord Jesus Christ returns.

[16] For the Lord himself shall descend from heaven with a shout, with the voice of the archangel, and

with the trump of God: and the dead in Christ shall rise first:

[17] Then we which are alive and remain shall be caught up together with them in the clouds, to meet the Lord in the air: and so shall we ever be with the Lord.

[18] Wherefore comfort one another with these words.

What an awesome hope! Our hope – the return of our Lord and Savior Jesus Christ! He came the first time a little over 2000 years ago, and he is returning. It could be tonight. It may not be for another 100 years, but he is coming back!

I Corinthians 15:51-58

[51] Behold, I shew you a mystery; We shall not all sleep, but we shall all be changed,

[52] In a moment, in the twinkling of an eye, at the last trump: for the trumpet shall sound, and the dead shall be raised incorruptible, and we shall be changed.

[53] For this corruptible [those that have died] must put on incorruption, and this mortal [those that are still alive at the return of Jesus Christ] must put on immortality.

[54] So when this corruptible shall have put on incorruption, and this mortal shall have put on immortality, then shall be brought to pass the saying that is written, Death is swallowed up in victory.

[55] O death, where is thy sting? O grave, where is thy victory?

[56] The sting of death is sin; and the strength of sin is the law.

[57] But thanks be to God, which giveth us the victory through our Lord Jesus Christ.

[58] Therefore, my beloved brethren, be ye stedfast, unmoveable, always abounding in the work of the Lord, forasmuch as ye know that your labour is not in vain in the Lord.

What a magnificent hope we look forward to! Jesus Christ most surely shall return! Because of our hope we are to be steadfast, unmovable, always abounding in the work of the Lord.

Why is there an urgency to our time? Well, it is not any more urgent than it has been since the day of Pentecost. The days are always crucial because time is limited. The Lord Jesus Christ could return at any moment – and when he does return, this administration of the Age of God's Grace will end. In other words, the door of the ark will be shut. When Christ returns this age of grace will be over.

This age of God's Grace has made it possible for mankind to receive God's spirit – to become sons of God and to receive eternal life. This sonship is available through believing that God raised Jesus Christ from the dead and confessing Jesus as lord of your life. (See Romans 10:9, 10)

Your sonship in Christ has nothing to do with how good or how bad you may have been. It has everything to do with the goodness of God and the completed work of Jesus Christ.

Your good works come into play after receiving the spirit of God in the new birth by grace. There are eternal rewards based upon your works after having received God's spirit.

It is clearly obvious we live in a crooked and perverse world. Evil is called good and good is called evil.

II Timothy refers to this time.

II Timothy 3:1-5

[1] This know also, that in the last days perilous times shall come.

[2] For men shall be lovers of their own selves, covetous, boasters, proud, blasphemers, disobedient to parents, unthankful, unholy,

[3] Without natural affection, trucebreakers, false accusers, incontinent, fierce, despisers of those that are good,

[4] Traitors, heady, highminded, lovers of pleasures more than lovers of God;

[5] Having a form of godliness, but denying the power thereof: from such turn away.

There is an urgency to our day, no different than it was in Acts 5:27-29 or in Acts 8:1-4.

There is an urgency for the unsaved: your coworker, neighbor or family member. Many live with no hope in this world. We must give them the opportunity to know God as their loving Heavenly Father.

There is an urgency for you: that you become steadfast, unmovable, always abounding in the work of the Lord because you know your labor is not in vain in the Lord!

There is an urgency for our country and world: it is in a death spiral because of the ongoing marginalization of God and His Word, and at times, the outright rejection of His grace and love. Unfortunately, the day is swiftly approaching, if it is not already here, where man's law will state you cannot speak of God's love and grace or mention the name of Jesus.

The name of Jesus Christ is the most powerful name in all of God's creation. The name of Jesus Christ saves the unsaved, heals the sick, casts out devil spirits, brings joy and peace to the mentally unstable. It is the name above all names. It is the name that all will confess as Lord, and every knee shall bow – either now or at the resurrection of the just and unjust.

Ask your Heavenly Father to show you who you really are. See your purpose.

There is an urgency to our times today like never before!

The door of the ark is still wide-open – it has not been closed yet!

Discussion Questions

1. What was the mystery hidden in God until it was revealed to the Apostle Paul?

2. How big is the Grace of God? List scripture verses that illustrate God's grace.

3. Who is the god of this world? What will open the eyes of those that are blinded by the god of this world?

4. What is your hope as detailed in I Thessalonians 4 and I Corinthians 15? While you wait for that hope what should you be abounding in?

5. Why is there an urgency of time for everyone?

CHAPTER 3

Do You Know Your Purpose?

D o you know your purpose in life? The Bible says our primary purpose in life is to seek first the kingdom of God and His righteousness. We are to worship, serve and love the one true God – our Heavenly Father.

Today we will narrow down our purpose practically into day-to-day living. You will see your purpose in life within the context of a relationship with God being the desire of your heart, God as the first love of your life.

Let's begin in II Corinthians.

II Corinthians 5:14, 15

[14] For the love of Christ constraineth us; [Constrain is an indepth heart request to live for Christ] because we thus judge, that if one [Jesus Christ] died for all, then were all dead:

[15] And that he [Jesus Christ] died for [in place of] all, that they which live should not henceforth live unto

themselves, but unto him which died for them, and rose again.

God gave you His son! Your natural response should be to live for Him.

There have been times throughout my life when others have helped me out when I had a need. Of myself, I didn't have the resources necessary to meet the obligation. Someone who did have the resources came along and supplied what was needed. I was extremely thankful and grateful for their kindness and gift!

It is not a man's sin that keeps him from God, it is the rejection of the savior, the Lord Jesus Christ that separates a man from God.

Look at the great gift God has given us in His son, the Lord Jesus Christ.

Because of the fall of man in the garden of Eden, Adam brought upon all mankind the sin nature. The result of Adam's disobedience was death – death in both the physical realm and in the spiritual. There became a debt that needed to be paid. The only one capable of paying that debt was the Lord Jesus Christ. We owe him our life.

Jesus did for us what we could never do for ourselves. It is not a man's sin that keeps him from God, it is the rejection of the savior, the Lord Jesus Christ that separates a man from God.

II Corinthians 5:21

²¹ For he [God] hath made him [Jesus Christ] to be sin for [in place of] us, who knew no sin; that we might be made the righteousness of God in him.

The word "knew" means to know by experience. Jesus Christ never experienced sin in his life. He did not receive the sin nature from Adam. He had perfect, sinless blood. He also never committed a sin. God made this perfect man, the Lord Jesus Christ, to be sin for us so that we could be made the righteousness of God.

You have the righteousness of God! It does not matter how bad or how good you have been – you still need Jesus Christ! Good works cannot save anyone. We all need to be redeemed from the sin nature that we have received through Adam.

God required a perfect sacrifice for man's redemption. Jesus Christ is that faultless man, the spotless sacrifice meeting all of God's requirements so that God could redeem mankind from the sin of Adam.

Because of the perfect work of Jesus Christ, God is now able to give you His spirit. God can now have a Father-child relationship with you.

In Romans chapter five, we see some wonderful truth regarding what we now have in Christ.

Romans 5:1

Therefore being justified by faith [by believing], we have peace with God through our Lord Jesus Christ:

The word "therefore" in verse one refers to chapter four where it speaks of Abraham and how he is the father of those who believe. Abraham believed the promise from God that he would be the father of many nations. He believed God's promise that he would have a child by Sarah, and that child would be the lineage from which man's redeemer would come.

In Romans 4:20, it states that "Abraham staggered not at the promise of God through unbelief; but was strong in faith [believing], giving glory to God." Abraham did not doubt the promise of God. The word "stagger" means to be divided in one's mind, to waver back and forth, to doubt.

In contrast to doubting God's promise, Abraham was strong in believing, giving glory to God!

Romans 4:21-25

[21] And being fully persuaded that, what he [God] had promised, he [God] was able also to perform.

[22] And therefore it was imputed [reckoned or set to his account] to him for righteousness.

[23] Now it was not written for his sake alone, that it was imputed to him;

[24] But for us also, to whom it shall be imputed [reckoned or set to our account], if we believe on him that raised up Jesus our Lord from the dead;

[25] Who was delivered for our offences, and was raised again for our justification.

Jesus Christ fulfilled God's requirement to redeem mankind.

Romans 5:1

> Therefore being justified by faith [by believing], we
> have peace with God through our Lord Jesus Christ:

Therefore – on account of Jesus Christ being raised for our
justification – we have peace with God through our Lord
Jesus Christ. You have peace with God! God is not mad at
you. He is not waiting to beat you over the head if you make
a mistake. You have peace with God.

Romans 5:6-10

> [6] For when we were yet without strength, in due time
> Christ died for the ungodly.

Christ died in place of the ungodly. He did not die when the
ungodly became good enough because of their works.

> [7] For scarcely for a righteous man will one die: yet
> peradventure for a good man some would even dare
> to die.

> [8] But God commendeth [shows] his love toward us, in
> that, while we were yet sinners, Christ died for us.

When we were sinners, Christ died for us or in place of us.
He did not die for you when your life was finally together.
No, he died for you when you were a sinner.

> [9] Much more then, being now justified by his blood,
> we shall be saved from wrath through him.

To be justified is to be declared legally righteous in the sight of God.

> [10] For if, when we were enemies, we were reconciled to God by the death of his Son, much more, being reconciled, we shall be saved by his life.

When you were an enemy of God, Jesus Christ died for you. We all were in a deeply sorry state – ungodly, sinners and enemies of God. Nevertheless, God in His love and mercy gave us a way of escape through the Lord Jesus Christ!

You have already been judged in Christ. In the judging, you have been found righteous. Jesus Christ did for you what you could never do for yourself. You are delivered from the coming wrath of God. The wrath of God for those who believe has been replaced with peace. You have peace with God.

Galatians 2:16, 19-21

> [16] Knowing that a man is not justified by the works of the law, but by the faith of Jesus Christ, even we have believed in Jesus Christ, that we might be justified by the faith of Christ, and not by the works of the law: for by the works of the law shall no flesh be justified.

Justification comes to you through the accomplished work of Jesus Christ. There are no works of the law that bring justification.

> [19] For I through the law am dead to the law, that I might live unto God.

How are we dead to the law? The book of Romans states, that Christ is the end of the law and that we have died with Christ.

> [20] I am crucified with Christ: nevertheless I live; yet not I, but Christ liveth in me: and the life which I now live in the flesh I live by the faith of the Son of God, who loved me, and gave himself for me.

> [21] I do not frustrate the grace of God: for if righteousness come by the law, then Christ is dead in vain.

If righteousness comes because of how good we are, then Christ died in vain. We do not frustrate the grace of God when we believe His Word, when we believe what He says about who we are in Christ.

We are to say, "Yes Father, thank you for all you have done for me through the accomplished work of Jesus Christ!" Hallelujah!

Romans 10:1-4

> [1] Brethren, my heart's desire and prayer to God for Israel is, that they might be saved.

Paul's heart for the children of Israel was God's heart for His people, that they might receive salvation.

> [2] For I bear them record that they have a zeal of God, but not according to knowledge.

³ For they being ignorant of God's righteousness, and going about to establish their own righteousness, have not submitted themselves unto the righteousness of God.

⁴ For Christ is the end of the law for righteousness to every one that believeth.

They had a religious zeal for God, but their zeal was not according to God's standard found in Christ. The children of Israel went about trying to earn God's righteousness by their good works. Jesus Christ totally fulfilled all that was required to redeem mankind.

Today some people try to stand righteous before God by their good works. Their effort is fruitless. Just as in the days of the early church they are ignorant of the righteousness found in Christ.

I Corinthians 1:30, 31

³⁰ But of him are ye in Christ Jesus, who of God is made unto us wisdom, and righteousness, and sanctification, and redemption:

³¹ That, according as it is written, He that glorieth, let him glory in the Lord.

You have wisdom. You are righteous. You have been set apart for God's purpose in your sanctification. You are redeemed.

We are to glory in the Lord, and all that He has done, we do not glory in our good works.

That is a long introduction, but it shows the essence – the heart, the depth – of why we live for our Father and His son, as we read earlier in II Corinthians 5:14, 15.

We can look at the book of Acts to see the standard of the Word living in the hearts and lives of God's people. God's Word is true! It is God's Word that sets our expectations for life!

Jesus Christ, before he ascended into heaven to claim his seat at the right hand of God, gave noticeably clear instruction.

Acts 1:8

But ye shall receive power, after that the Holy Ghost [holy spirit] is come upon you: and ye shall be witnesses unto me both in Jerusalem, and in all Judaea, and in Samaria, and unto the uttermost part of the earth.

The uttermost part of the earth includes where you are today! On the day of Pentecost, the apostles were a witness to the power of the holy spirit. The witness was revealed when they spoke in tongues.

The day of Pentecost and the giving of the holy spirit opened the great Age of God's Grace. In Acts chapter two, we read what Peter spoke in the temple to those in Jerusalem shortly after having received the gift of holy spirit.

Acts 2:38-41

[38] Then Peter said unto them, Repent, and be baptized every one of you in the name of Jesus Christ for the

remission of sins, and ye shall receive the gift of the Holy Ghost.

[39] For the promise is unto you, and to your children, and to all that are afar off, even as many as the Lord our God shall call.

[40] And with many other words did he testify and exhort, saying, Save yourselves from this untoward [crooked] generation.

[41] Then they that gladly received his word were baptized: and the same day there were added unto them about three thousand souls.

Wow! About 3000 people were added to the church on the day of Pentecost. They gladly received God's Word and were baptized with the holy spirit. They confessed Jesus as lord and they believed that God raised Jesus Christ from the dead. They received eternal life!

This next record in Acts chapter four takes place shortly after Peter and John healed the man who was born lame. It caused an uproar among the religious leaders.

Acts 4:7-20

[7] And when they had set them in the midst, they asked, By what power, or by what name, have ye done this?

[8] Then Peter, filled with the Holy Ghost [holy spirit], said unto them, Ye rulers of the people, and elders of Israel,

[9] If we this day be examined of the good deed done to the impotent man, by what means he is made whole;

[10] Be it known unto you all, and to all the people of Israel, that by the name of Jesus Christ of Nazareth, whom ye crucified, whom God raised from the dead, even by him doth this man stand here before you whole.

[11] This is the stone which was set at nought of you builders, which is become the head of the corner.

[12] Neither is there salvation in any other: for there is none other name under heaven given among men, whereby we must be saved.

Look at the boldness of Peter and John.

[13] Now when they saw the boldness of Peter and John, and perceived that they were unlearned and ignorant men, they marvelled; and they took knowledge of them, that they had been with Jesus.

Here "unlearned and ignorant" means that Peter and John did not have the right theological training. They did not go to seminary school! However, they had been with Jesus.

[14] And beholding the man which was healed standing with them, they could say nothing against it.

[15] But when they had commanded them to go aside out of the council, they conferred among themselves,

[16] Saying, What shall we do to these men? for that indeed a notable miracle hath been done by them is manifest to all them that dwell in Jerusalem; and we cannot deny it.

[17] But that it spread no further among the people, let us straitly threaten them, that they speak henceforth to no man in this name.

[18] And they called them, and commanded them not to speak at all nor teach in the name of Jesus.

[19] But Peter and John answered and said unto them, Whether it be right in the sight of God to hearken unto you more than unto God, judge ye.

[20] For we cannot but speak the things which we have seen and heard.

What a wonderful example Peter and John are for us today. God has not changed. His Word has not changed. God's Word brings deliverance and healing when His Word is believed. God is waiting for us to boldly speak and live for Him. When we do, we too will see great signs, miracles and wonders.

There is a tremendous record here in Acts chapter eight following the stoning of Stephen. The believers boldly speak God's Word!

Acts 8:1-4

[1] And Saul [later the Apostle Paul] was consenting unto his [Stephen's] death. And at that time there was

a great persecution against the church which was at
Jerusalem; and they were all scattered abroad
throughout the regions of Judaea and Samaria, except
the apostles.

The church being "scattered abroad" was not haphazard. It
was a very systematic purposeful movement. One family was
sent to Syria, another group to Phenice and another group to
Cyprus and so forth.

> [2] And devout men carried Stephen to his burial, and
> made great lamentation over him.
>
> [3] As for Saul, he made havock of the church, entering
> into every house, and haling [arresting] men and
> women committed them to prison.
>
> [4] Therefore they that were scattered abroad went
> every where preaching the word.

What did they preach? The Word of God! Did they talk
about the persecution and the hardship? No, they preached
God's Word. What a wonderful example they are to us today.

In Acts 11, we see an amazing record that refers to some of
those that were scattered abroad in Acts 8.

Acts 11:19-21

> [19] Now they which were scattered abroad upon the
> persecution that arose about Stephen travelled as far
> as Phenice, and Cyprus, and Antioch, [doing what?]
> preaching the word to none but unto the Jews only.

When they were scattered abroad, they went to Phenice, which was about 200 miles from Jerusalem. They went to Cyprus, about 270 miles from Jerusalem. They went to Antioch, about 320 miles from Jerusalem. In their travel, they did not have modern transportation like we have today. They used horses, carts, and their feet. They went no small distance. They did not complain about how hard it was and what a disruption it was to their lives. They spoke God's Word.

> [20] And some of them were men of Cyprus and Cyrene, which, when they were come to Antioch, spake unto the Grecians, preaching the Lord Jesus.

> [21] And the hand of the Lord was with them: and a great number believed, and turned unto the Lord.

What a wonderful example of believing and speaking God's Word we see here in Acts 11. Another example that speaks loudly to us today is found in Acts 19.

Acts 19:8-12, 20

> [8] And he went into the synagogue, and spake boldly for the space of three months, disputing and persuading the things concerning the kingdom of God.

> [9] But when divers were hardened, and believed not, but spake evil of that way before the multitude, he departed from them, and separated the disciples, disputing daily in the school of one Tyrannus.

[10] And this continued by the space of two years; so that all they which dwelt in Asia heard the word of the Lord Jesus, both Jews and Greeks.

[11] And God wrought special miracles by the hands of Paul:

[12] So that from his body were brought unto the sick handkerchiefs or aprons, and the diseases departed from them, and the evil spirits went out of them.

[20] So mightily grew the word of God and prevailed.

What started out in the synagogue, and then moved to the school of Tyrannus over a period of two years and three months, resulted in all of Asia hearing the wonderful truth regarding the Lord Jesus Christ. This remarkable move of God's Word started with just twelve men. It resulted in an untold number – thousands or millions of people – becoming born again, to the end that all which dwelt in Asia heard the word of the Lord Jesus, both Jews and Greeks.

God has not changed. It is available today for all of Asia to hear the Word of God. It is attainable today for all of the United States, all of Mexico, all of Russia, all of _____; you fill in the blank, to hear the Word of God. All it takes is men and women like you who are willing to speak God's Word and love with God's love, no matter the opposition.

Today, it is not "PC," or politically correct to talk about God or speak of the Lord Jesus Christ. I would much rather have us be "BC," or Biblically correct, and speak God's Word boldly! If some get offended, fine. The unbelievers in the days of Christ were offended too! And you just might find that some of the opposition end up believing and becoming wonderful saints for the one true God, just as Saul became the great Apostle Paul.

Many would love to see a revival of the magnitude that the first century church experienced. God has not changed. God is just as loving, mighty and powerful today as He was in the days of the Apostles. His Word is still the same – yesterday, today and forever. It is God's Word believed that changes the heart and life of a man or a woman. Our heart should be one of "here am I, send me!"

People everywhere, every day are grasping for hope in this hopeless world. Their hearts cry out for love. Share God's Word and His love wherever you are, because God has given you the privilege to reconcile to Him those that hunger and thirst for righteousness. They are out there, and they cross your path every day.

Your purpose is found in Christ and Christ alone!

Discussion Questions

1. What does God instruct us to seek first? Why?

2. Is the righteousness you have received from God dependent upon your good works? Document your answer with a Bible verse.

3. In Acts chapter 8 after the stoning of Stephen the believers went everywhere preaching the Word of God. How might you apply their example to a negative circumstance you may be facing in your life?

4. Your purpose in life is found in Christ. What is God working in your heart and life today?

CHAPTER 4

God is Light

Think of the last time you walked into a totally dark room and turned on a light. When the light comes on the darkness flees. You can see where you are going.

Can darkness ever extinguish the light? No. Can the darkness ever chase away the light? No. Light will ALWAYS remove the darkness.

We know this is true in the physical realm. Every night when the sun sets, we turn on the lights.

What else does light do? It allows us to see clearly. It lights our path so that we do not stumble or fall. Light enables us not to get hurt.

I remember once walking into a totally pitch-black room at work. I knew the light switch was about 20 feet away across the room. I began to walk toward the switch not knowing there was a pile of boards in the middle of the room. I tripped and fell. Thankfully, the fall did not seriously injure me. I eventually turned the light on, and I could then see the danger in the middle of the room.

We know the benefit of using light in the natural realm.

It is no different when it comes to spiritual matters. There is a very real spiritual world. In the spiritual realm, there is both light and darkness.

I John 1:5

This then is the message which we have heard of him, and declare unto you, that God is light, and in him is no darkness at all.

God is light and in Him there is NO darkness!

In our society and culture, both light and darkness are attributed to God. You will hear people say that God made someone sick to make them humbler. When someone dies, they may say that God took them home to be with Him; or they may think the mighty storm that brought devastation upon a city is God's judgment upon that city. All that thinking is a lie – it is not true. It cannot be true if God's Word is true.

Sickness, death, and devastating storms are all darkness. God says of Himself here in I John that He is light and in Him is no darkness at all.

For thousands of years God's arch enemy, the devil, has been a master at hiding and deceiving. He has convinced people that his dark works are the work of the one true God.

The light of God's Word dispels the lies of darkness.

Here is the truth of God's Word – God is light and in Him is NO darkness!

God does not bring sickness, death, or storms. He is light.

Jesus Christ said that he always did his Father's will. If we look then at what Jesus Christ did, we can know the will of the Father. The life of Jesus Christ makes known the will of God.

John 8:28, 29

28 Then said Jesus unto them, When ye have lifted up the Son of man, then shall ye know that I am he, and that I do nothing of myself; but as my Father hath taught me, I speak these things.

29 And he that sent me is with me: the Father hath not left me alone; for I do always those things that please him.

Here in John eight, Jesus Christ said that the Father was always with him, and that he always did those acts which pleased his Father. So, if we want to find out that which we can attribute to God then we must look at the works of Jesus Christ.

In the Gospels we see some of those works.

Matthew 4:23, 24

23 And Jesus went about all Galilee, teaching in their synagogues, and preaching the gospel of the kingdom, and healing all manner of sickness and all manner of disease among the people.

24 And his fame went throughout all Syria: and they brought unto him all sick people that were taken with

> divers diseases and torments, and those which were
> possessed with devils, and those which were lunatick,
> and those that had the palsy; and he healed them.

Jesus healed every kind of sickness and disease. Jesus cast out
devil spirits from those that were possessed.

Matthew 8:16

> When the even was come, they brought unto him
> many that were possessed with devils: and he cast out
> the spirits with his word, and healed all that were sick:

He healed all that were sick. He did not tell any, "No, I can't
heal you today. It is not God's will." He healed all that were
sick. Here we see the will of God through the life of Jesus
Christ. God's will is for you to be healthy.

Luke 7:21, 22

> [21] And in that same hour he cured many of their
> infirmities and plagues, and of evil spirits; and unto
> many that were blind he gave sight.

> [22] Then Jesus answering said unto them, Go your way,
> and tell John what things ye have seen and heard;
> how that the blind see, the lame walk, the lepers are
> cleansed, the deaf hear, the dead are raised, to the
> poor the gospel is preached.

Once again, we see God's will for His people; that they be
healed; that they be delivered.

Matthew 8:23-26

²³ And when he was entered into a ship, his disciples followed him.

²⁴ And, behold, there arose a great tempest in the sea, insomuch that the ship was covered with the waves: but he was asleep.

²⁵ And his disciples came to him, and awoke him, saying, Lord, save us: we perish.

²⁶ And he saith unto them, Why are ye fearful, O ye of little faith [believing]? Then he arose, and rebuked the winds and the sea; and there was a great calm.

We can read record after record after record of the works of light that Jesus Christ did. He always did his Father's will. He only did what his Father showed him. He healed the sick. He raised the dead. He calmed the storm.

Not once did Jesus make someone sick to make them humble. Never did he kill someone to take them home to be with the Father. Never did he generate a storm to bring judgment upon a people.

Acts 10:38

How God anointed Jesus of Nazareth with the Holy Ghost and with power: who went about doing good, and healing all that were oppressed of the devil; for God was with him.

There it is, clear as day: sickness, death and storms are oppression from the adversary, the devil. They are the devil's works of darkness. God is light. In Him is no darkness at all.

Acts 2:22

Ye men of Israel, hear these words; Jesus of Nazareth, a man approved of God among you by miracles and wonders and signs, which God did by him in the midst of you, as ye yourselves also know:

God approved of the works of Jesus Christ. God showed His approval by raising him from the dead. God approved of the healing, the raising of the dead and the calming of the storm.

Psalm 119:130

The entrance of thy words giveth light; it giveth understanding unto the simple.

We are reading here the Words of light. They dispel darkness from our thinking and understanding. God's Word raises our expectation for deliverance. God's truth enables us to believe, to receive all the goodness that our Heavenly Father has in store for us today — not someday, not tomorrow – today!

Psalm 119:105

Thy word is a lamp unto my feet, and a light unto my path.

God's Word lights our path so we may live an abundant life. It shows us what to think. It dispels the darkness from the crevices of our mind. It makes manifest lies we may have believed. God's Word cleanses our heart. His Word is the light that illuminates our path in life.

Why would it be so important to guard our thinking? Why would it be crucial for each of us that we allow the entrance of God's Word to shine in our mind and heart?

Proverbs 4:18-23

[18] But the path of the just is as the shining light, that shineth more and more unto the perfect day.

[19] The way of the wicked is as darkness: they know not at what they stumble.

[20] My son, attend to my words; incline thine ear unto my sayings.

[21] Let them [God's Words] not depart from thine eyes; keep them in the midst of thine heart.

[22] For they are life unto those that find them, and health to all their flesh.

[23] Keep thy heart with all diligence; for out of it [out of the heart] are the issues of life.

The word "keep" in verse 23 means to guard; to guard our hearts with all diligence. "With all diligence" literally could be translated "above all that is kept, above all things else." We are to guard our hearts.

How do we guard our hearts? We guard our hearts by controlling our thinking. We are to keep or guard our heart with all diligence. For out of it, the heart, are the issues of life.

What are the issues of life? The issues of life are who you are. The issues of life are what you live. The heart is the source of your life lived. That is why it is so important for us to guard our thinking. That is why we must put on the light of God's Word. We are to read God's Word and meditate on His Word. When we talk to our loving, gracious, heavenly Father about His Word, He opens the eyes of our understanding. When you read His Word, ask Him to show you the great gems of truth that He has for you.

> We are to keep or guard our heart with all diligence. For out of it, the heart, are the issues of life.

John 12:42-50

[42] Nevertheless among the chief rulers also many believed on him; but because of the Pharisees they did not confess him, lest they should be put out of the synagogue:

[43] For they loved the praise of men more than the praise of God.

Never live for the praise of men. Live for the praise of God. Man's praise is temporary and always has strings attached. God is steadfast and faithful. His approval lasts for eternity.

[44] Jesus cried and said, He that believeth on me, believeth not on me, but on him that sent me.

⁴⁵ And he that seeth me seeth him that sent me.

⁴⁶ I am come a light into the world, that whosoever believeth on me should not abide in darkness.

Jesus Christ said of himself that he is a light that came into the world. Whosoever should believe on Him would not live in darkness.

⁴⁷ And if any man hear my words, and believe not, I judge him not: for I came not to judge the world, but to save the world.

⁴⁸ He that rejecteth me, and receiveth not my words, hath one that judgeth him: the word that I have spoken, the same shall judge him in the last day.

⁴⁹ For I have not spoken of myself; but the Father which sent me, he gave me a commandment, what I should say, and what I should speak.

⁵⁰ And I know that his commandment is life everlasting: whatsoever I speak therefore, even as the Father said unto me, so I speak.

Jesus Christ lived the heart of his Father. He made known the Father by his works, by the words that he spoke. His life dispelled darkness.

We see God's heart through the life of Jesus Christ. He healed people. He raised people from the dead. He calmed the mighty storm. God is light and in Him there is no darkness at all!

Philippians 2:5-16

⁵ Let this mind be in you, which was also in Christ Jesus:

We can have the mind of Christ as we think God's Word.

⁶ Who, being in the form of God, thought it not robbery to be equal [agree] with God:

⁷ But made himself of no reputation, and took upon him the form of a servant, and was made in the likeness of men:

⁸ And being found in fashion as a man, he humbled himself, and became obedient unto death, even the death of the cross.

⁹ Wherefore God also hath highly exalted him, and given him a name which is above every name:

¹⁰ That at the name of Jesus every knee should bow, of things in heaven, and things in earth, and things under the earth;

¹¹ And that every tongue should confess that Jesus Christ is Lord, to the glory of God the Father.

What a wonderful example Jesus Christ is for us in his obedience to his heavenly Father. He was obedient all the way unto death. He believed that his Father would raise him from the dead. He gave his life so that we could have life.

¹² Wherefore, my beloved, as ye have always obeyed, not as in my presence only, but now much more in

my absence, work out [demonstrate] your own
salvation [wholeness] with fear [respect] and
trembling [obedience].

[13] For it is God which worketh in you both to will and
to do of his good pleasure.

God works within you to will and to do His good pleasure.
God directs the heart of a person whose heart desires to do
His will. The thoughts, the desires, the passions to serve and
give are a result of God working within you.

[14] Do all things without murmurings and disputings:

What are those things we are to do without murmuring and
disputing? The things that God works within. What an
amazing privilege! What an awesomely wonderful truth to
know that the Creator of the heavens and the earth works
within us to will and to do of His good pleasure.

[15] That ye may be blameless and harmless, the sons of
God, without rebuke, in the midst of a crooked and
perverse nation, among whom ye shine as lights in the
world;

Remember that God is light and in Him is no darkness at all.
You have His light shining in your heart and life. You are the
one that shines as a light in the world. Just as Jesus Christ
healed people, raised the dead and calmed the storm, so you
too can do the same. You are the light in this dark and
perverse world.

¹⁶ Holding forth the word of life; that I may rejoice in the day of Christ, that I have not run in vain, neither laboured in vain.

You will not have run in vain or labored in vain when you live that which God works within you!

Ephesians 2:10

For we are his workmanship, created in Christ Jesus unto good works, which God hath before ordained that we should walk in them.

You are God's workmanship. You are created in Christ Jesus unto good works. What are those good works? Those good works are the works of Philippians 2:13 that the spirit of God works within you. God prepared for you to walk in them.

You are a child of light, and you shine as light in this world. Allow God to work within you both to will and to do of His good pleasure.

God is light and in Him is no darkness at all!

Discussion Questions

1. Jesus Christ stated in the Gospel of John that he always did his Father's will. What are some of the things that Jesus Christ did?

2. Why was Jesus Christ able to heal all that were oppressed of the devil?

3. God's Word is light. Why is it profitable for you to read and understand God's Word?

4. How do you guard your heart? Give an example when you recently saw the light of God's Word dispel darkness in your life.

5. Philippians 2:13 states that "God works within you to will and to do of His good pleasure." What has God been working in your heart? What are some of the good works that He has prepared for you to do?

CHAPTER 5

The Father of Mercy – The God of All Comfort

II Corinthians 1:3

Blessed be God, even the Father of our Lord Jesus Christ, the Father of mercies, and the God of all comfort;

God is the Father of mercy. What is it to be merciful? Mercy has been defined as the withholding of earned judgment. Mercy certainly is that! Often you will see in God's Word both mercy and grace together. Grace is God's unearned favor.

We have done nothing of ourselves to earn either God's mercy or His grace. He is merciful and He is gracious because He is love. The mercy of God is also displayed in compassion.

It is always appropriate to look at the life of Jesus Christ and his example to see the heart of the Father, to see the heart of our God – the Father of mercy and the God of all comfort.

Matthew 14:13, 14

[13] When Jesus heard of it, he departed thence by ship into a desert place apart: and when the people had heard thereof, they followed him on foot out of the cities.

[14] And Jesus went forth, and saw a great multitude, and was moved with compassion toward them, and he healed their sick.

This was immediately after Jesus learned of the death of John the Baptist. His forerunner, the great prophet whom Jesus called the one greatest among men born of a woman, had just been beheaded. John the Baptist was Jesus Christ's cousin. Can you imagine Jesus' heart? He knew what the life of John the Baptist meant to his Father. He knew what John's life meant to the children of Israel. Now, John was brutally murdered.

Jesus saw the great multitude, and his heart was moved with compassion toward them. He healed their sick! That is a shining example of God's mercy and His comfort in action.

John 8:2-11

[2] And early in the morning he came again into the temple, and all the people came unto him; and he sat down, and taught them.

[3] And the scribes and Pharisees brought unto him a woman taken in adultery; and when they had set her in the midst,

[4] They say unto him, Master, this woman was taken in adultery, in the very act.

[5] Now Moses in the law commanded us, that such should be stoned: but what sayest thou?

[6] This they said, tempting him, that they might have to accuse him. But Jesus stooped down, and with his finger wrote on the ground, as though he heard them not.

[7] So when they continued asking him, he lifted up himself, and said unto them, He that is without sin among you, let him first cast a stone at her.

[8] And again he stooped down, and wrote on the ground.

[9] And they which heard it, being convicted by their own conscience, went out one by one, beginning at the eldest, even unto the last: and Jesus was left alone, and the woman standing in the midst.

[10] When Jesus had lifted up himself, and saw none but the woman, he said unto her, Woman, where are those thine accusers? hath no man condemned thee?

[11] She said, No man, Lord. And Jesus said unto her, Neither do I condemn thee: go, and sin no more.

What mercy! What compassion! Men are so often quick to judge and bring condemnation upon another. In this situation, Jesus was the only one without sin among them. He is the only one that could have cast a stone. He did not. He loved her, and in his words, "neither do I condemn thee, go and sin no more." That is the boundless mercy of God.

John 13:1

Now before the feast of the passover, when Jesus knew that his hour was come that he should depart out of this world unto the Father, having loved his own which were in the world, he loved them unto the end.

The word "end" is an interesting word. It means he loved them completely. It is not so much talking about *the end* as it pertains to time. It is referring to the end of doing whatever it took. He was obedient to his Father all the way unto the end. Jesus had a heart of service. He gave people God's love and God's Word, God's mercy and God's compassion. He held nothing back; he loved them unto the end. He did all that was required.

In the Old Testament, there are many, many examples of God's abundant mercy toward His people. Time and time again the children of Israel rebelled against God … and … time and time again God extended His mercy toward His people.

Nehemiah 9:16, 17, 28, 31

[16] But they and our fathers dealt proudly, and hardened their necks, and hearkened not to thy commandments,

¹⁷ And refused to obey, neither were mindful of thy wonders that thou didst among them; but hardened their necks, and in their rebellion appointed a captain to return to their bondage: but thou art a God ready to pardon, gracious and merciful, slow to anger, and of great kindness, and forsookest them not.

²⁸ But after they had rest, they did evil again before thee: therefore leftest thou them in the land of their enemies, so that they had the dominion over them: yet when they returned, and cried unto thee, thou heardest them from heaven; and many times didst thou deliver them according to thy mercies;

³¹ Nevertheless for thy great mercies' sake thou didst not utterly consume them, nor forsake them; for thou art a gracious and merciful God.

The children of Israel refused to obey God. In their rebellion, they appointed someone to lead them back to their bondage. That is insane, but that is what happens when people do not recognize the abundant grace and the rich mercy of God.

Nevertheless, God was willing to pardon the children of Israel. He was gracious. He was merciful, slow to anger, and of great kindness. He did not forsake His people.

Deuteronomy 7:9

Know therefore that the Lord thy God, he is God, the faithful God, which keepeth covenant and mercy with them that love him and keep his commandments to a thousand generations;

God is not only merciful, but He is a faithful God. He keeps His Word.

God is not only merciful, but He is a faithful God. He keeps His Word.

God does not lie. He does not misrepresent His intentions; He does not say one thing and mean another. He is a faithful God, He is merciful, He is willing to pardon and forgive. God has shown the greatness of His mercy through the life of Jesus Christ. There is absolutely nothing we did to earn God's mercy and grace. We have a very loving and kind heavenly Father.

In Psalms, we see many examples of God's mercy.

Psalm 25:6-10

⁶ Remember, O Lord, thy tender mercies and thy lovingkindnesses; for they have been ever of old.

⁷ Remember not the sins of my youth, nor my transgressions: according to thy mercy remember thou me for thy goodness' sake, O Lord.

⁸ Good and upright is the Lord: therefore will he teach sinners in the way.

⁹ The meek will he guide in judgment: and the meek will he teach his way.

¹⁰ All the paths of the Lord are mercy and truth unto such as keep his covenant and his testimonies.

Psalm 86:3-5, 15

[3] Be merciful unto me, O Lord: for I cry unto thee daily.

[4] Rejoice the soul of thy servant: for unto thee, O Lord, do I lift up my soul.

[5] For thou, Lord, art good, and ready to forgive; and plenteous in mercy unto all them that call upon thee.

[15] But thou, O Lord, art a God full of compassion, and gracious, long suffering, and plenteous in mercy and truth.

Wow! We have an amazing God! We have an awesome Father, and He is the Father of all mercy.

Psalm 136 speaks of the mercy of God.

Psalm 136:1-26

[1] O give thanks unto the Lord; for he is good: for his **mercy** endureth for ever.

[2] O give thanks unto the God of gods: for his **mercy** endureth for ever.

[3] O give thanks to the Lord of lords: for his **mercy** endureth for ever.

[4] To him who alone doeth great wonders: for his **mercy** endureth for ever.

[5] To him that by wisdom made the heavens: for his **mercy** endureth for ever.

⁶ To him that stretched out the earth above the waters: for his **mercy** endureth for ever.

⁷ To him that made great lights: for his **mercy** endureth for ever:

⁸ The sun to rule by day: for his **mercy** endureth for ever:

⁹ The moon and stars to rule by night: for his **mercy** endureth for ever.

¹⁰ To him that smote Egypt in their firstborn: for his **mercy** endureth for ever:

¹¹ And brought out Israel from among them: for his **mercy** endureth for ever:

¹² With a strong hand, and with a stretched out arm: for his **mercy** endureth for ever.

¹³ To him which divided the Red sea into parts: for his **mercy** endureth for ever:

¹⁴ And made Israel to pass through the midst of it: for his **mercy** endureth for ever:

¹⁵ But overthrew Pharaoh and his host in the Red sea: for his **mercy** endureth for ever.

¹⁶ To him which led his people through the wilderness: for his **mercy** endureth for ever.

¹⁷ To him which smote great kings: for his **mercy** endureth for ever:

[18] And slew famous kings: for his **mercy** endureth for ever:

[19] Sihon king of the Amorites: for his **mercy** endureth for ever:

[20] And Og the king of Bashan: for his **mercy** endureth for ever:

[21] And gave their land for an heritage: for his **mercy** endureth for ever:

[22] Even an heritage unto Israel his servant: for his **mercy** endureth for ever.

[23] Who remembered us in our low estate: for his **mercy** endureth for ever:

[24] And hath redeemed us from our enemies: for his **mercy** endureth for ever.

[25] Who giveth food to all flesh: for his **mercy** endureth for ever.

[26] O give thanks unto the God of heaven: for his **mercy** endureth for ever.

God's mercies abound in every aspect of His wisdom and in His heart for His people.

Psalm 138:8

The Lord will perfect that which concerneth me: thy mercy, O Lord, endureth for ever: forsake not the works of thine own hands.

Psalm 145:9

The Lord is good to all: and his tender mercies are over all his works.

In the gospels, we can read of the Lord Jesus Christ displaying the mercy of God by his compassion toward others.

In the New Testament, we see many truths regarding God's mercy.

Romans 12:1

I beseech you therefore, brethren, by the mercies of God, that ye present your bodies a living sacrifice, holy, acceptable unto God, which is your reasonable service.

In response to God's mercy, we are to present ourselves a living sacrifice. We are to live for God. That is our reasonable and logical duty.

Ephesians 2:4-9

[4] But God, who is rich in mercy, for his great love wherewith he loved us,

[5] Even when we were dead in sins, hath quickened us together with Christ, (by grace ye are saved;)

[6] And hath raised us up together, and made us sit together in heavenly places in Christ Jesus:

[7] That in the ages to come he might shew the exceeding riches of his grace in his kindness toward us through Christ Jesus.

[8] For by grace are ye saved through faith; and that not of yourselves: it is the gift of God:

[9] Not of works, lest any man should boast.

Please do not ever think that God does not love you. Please do not think that you are not good enough for God. He is rich in His mercy. Mercy is compassionate; mercy loves. God has no shortage of loving kindness to show toward you.

Hebrews 4:15, 16

[15] For we have not an high priest which cannot be touched with the feeling of our infirmities; but was in all points tempted like as we are, yet without sin.

[16] Let us therefore come boldly unto the throne of grace, that we may obtain mercy, and find grace to help in time of need.

It is in our time of need that we come boldly, or confidently, unto the throne of grace. God is more than willing to meet you where you are. It does not say that we are to come boldly to the throne of grace when we have our life together. It says we are to come boldly in our time of need.

II Corinthians 1:3

Blessed be God, even the Father of our Lord Jesus Christ, the Father of mercies, and the God of all comfort;

It is a comfort to know that our Heavenly Father is compassionate and merciful. As David said in Psalms, let each of us say today: "Be merciful unto me, O God, be merciful unto me: For my soul trusts in thee!"

Discussion Questions

1. What is mercy?

2. List three examples of God's mercy in the Old Testament.

3. Give an example where Jesus Christ showed mercy towards another. Where has God shown you mercy?

4. Romans 12:1 states "that you are to present your body a living sacrifice." How is His mercy encouraging you to live for Him.

CHAPTER 6

The Name of Jesus Christ

Jesus Christ is the most powerful name on earth and in heaven. It is a name not to be taken lightly. It is the name that God has given to His children to speak in any circumstance, for it is the name of Jesus Christ that is above all names!

Philippians 2:8-11

[8] And being found in fashion as a man, he humbled himself, and became obedient unto death, even the death of the cross.

[9] Wherefore God also hath highly exalted him, and given him a name which is above every name:

[10] That at the name of Jesus every knee should bow, of things in heaven, and things in earth, and things under the earth;

[11] And that every tongue should confess that Jesus Christ is Lord, to the glory of God the Father.

Jesus Christ humbled himself and became obedient unto death, even the death of the cross. God then highly exalted him and gave him a name which is above every name.

His name is above every name! The name of Jesus Christ is above the name of cancer. His name is above the name of depression. The name of Jesus is above the name of Covid. The name of Jesus is above the name of allergies. The name of Jesus is above the name of any ailment or sickness. His name is above the name of death. His name is above calamities and storms.

His name is above all names!

Have you ever noticed the reaction of people when the name of Jesus Christ is spoken in public? Some may shout, "Halleluiah!" Others bow their head in reverence. Some act as if they did not hear it and move away. Some may scowl. The name of Jesus will always cause a reaction from the hearer – sometimes positive, sometimes negative.

Why is that? There is a spiritual battle in this world. It is hidden to most. The weapons in the battle are words – The Word of God versus the words of the adversary, the devil.

No matter what the skirmish in life, God's Word will always triumph when spoken on the believing lips of a Christian. Of all the words available, the most effective and mighty are found in the name of Jesus Christ!

Acts 4:10-12

¹⁰ Be it known unto you all, and to all the people of Israel, that by the name of Jesus Christ of Nazareth, whom ye crucified, whom God raised from the dead, even by him doth this man stand here before you whole.

¹¹ This is the stone which was set at nought of you builders, which is become the head of the corner.

¹² Neither is there salvation in any other: for there is none other name under heaven given among men, whereby we must be saved.

There is no other name under heaven, given among men, whereby we must be saved.

The name of Jesus Christ is above all names.

Buddha cannot save anyone. Krishna cannot save anyone. Mohammad cannot save anyone. All the Hindu gods cannot save anyone. Money and good works cannot buy salvation.

It is only by the name of Jesus Christ that eternal salvation is found. It is in that name of Jesus that a man, woman, or child can go from being dead in trespasses and sins to being eternally saved, marked out to spend all eternity with the one true God!

In Acts chapter two, shortly after the giving of the gift of holy spirit on the day of Pentecost, Peter spoke what is recorded in the following verses.

Acts 2:38, 39

[38] Then Peter said unto them, Repent, and be baptized every one of you in the name of Jesus Christ for the remission of sins, and ye shall receive the gift of the Holy Ghost.

[39] For the promise is unto you, and to your children, and to all that are afar off, even as many as the Lord our God shall call.

God is calling you. Jesus Christ gave his life for you, so that you could receive the gift of holy spirit.

In Acts chapter four, the rulers called Peter, John and the apostles and commanded them not to speak the name of Jesus.

Acts 4:17-20

[17] But that it spread no further among the people, let us straitly threaten them, that they speak henceforth to no man in this name.

[18] And they called them, and commanded them not to speak at all nor teach in the name of Jesus.

[19] But Peter and John answered and said unto them, Whether it be right in the sight of God to hearken unto you more than unto God, judge ye.

[20] For we cannot but speak the things which we have seen and heard.

The religious leaders threatened Peter and John. The leaders told them not to speak the name of Jesus Christ. Look at the reaction that name causes! There is great benefit for those who believe in that name! There are severe consequences for those that do not. After Peter and John were released by the authorities they went back to the believers and they prayed. Look at what they prayed.

Acts 4:29-33

[29] And now, Lord, behold their threatenings: and grant unto thy servants, that with all boldness they may speak thy word,

[30] By stretching forth thine hand to heal; and that signs and wonders may be done by the name of thy holy child Jesus.

What got them into trouble was speaking God's Word, preaching, and healing by the name of Jesus Christ. They were operating the power and utilizing the authority that is found in that name. What did they do when they returned to the brethren? They asked for more boldness to speak God's Word!

In Acts 5, the apostles were thrown in prison for speaking the name of Jesus.

Acts 5:15, 16

[15] Insomuch that they brought forth the sick into the streets, and laid them on beds and couches, that at the least the shadow of Peter passing by might overshadow some of them.

[16] There came also a multitude out of the cities round about unto Jerusalem, bringing sick folks, and them which were vexed with unclean spirits: and they were healed every one.

No one was missed in the healing. They all were healed! It is God's Will that you be healthy!

Acts 5:17-29

[17] Then the high priest rose up, and all they that were with him, (which is the sect of the Sadducees,) and were filled with indignation,

[18] And laid their hands on the apostles, and put them in the common prison.

[19] But the angel of the Lord by night opened the prison doors, and brought them forth, and said,

[20] Go, stand and speak in the temple to the people all the words of this life.

[21] And when they heard that, they entered into the temple early in the morning, and taught. But the high priest came, and they that were with him, and called the council together, and all the senate of the children

of Israel, and sent to the prison to have them brought.

[22] But when the officers came, and found them not in the prison, they returned and told,

[23] Saying, The prison truly found we shut with all safety, and the keepers standing without before the doors: but when we had opened, we found no man within.

[24] Now when the high priest and the captain of the temple and the chief priests heard these things, they doubted of them whereunto this would grow.

[25] Then came one and told them, saying, Behold, the men whom ye put in prison are standing in the temple, and teaching the people.

[26] Then went the captain with the officers, and brought them without violence: for they feared the people, lest they should have been stoned.

[27] And when they had brought them, they set them before the council: and the high priest asked them,

[28] Saying, Did not we straitly command you that ye should not teach in this name? and, behold, ye have filled Jerusalem with your doctrine, and intend to bring this man's blood upon us.

[29] Then Peter and the other apostles answered and said, We ought to obey God rather than men.

Peter and the apostle's only appropriate response to the accusation brought against them was, "we ought to obey God rather than men." Once again, they got into "trouble" by speaking the name of Jesus Christ and healing people in that name.

Acts 5:41, 42

[41] And they departed from the presence of the council, rejoicing that they were counted worthy to suffer shame for his name.

[42] And daily in the temple, and in every house, they ceased not to teach and preach Jesus Christ.

It is that name of Jesus Christ that will cause men and women to have to decide! Do you believe in the salvation and wholeness which are found in his name? Or do you despise and reject that name? Each of us must make that decision. Each of us receives the benefits or consequences of that decision.

Acts 8:5-8

[5] Then Philip went down to the city of Samaria, and preached Christ unto them.

[6] And the people with one accord gave heed unto those things which Philip spake, hearing and seeing the miracles which he did.

[7] For unclean spirits, crying with loud voice, came out of many that were possessed with them: and many taken with palsies, and that were lame, were healed.

⁸ And there was great joy in that city.

There was great joy in Samaria. It is the name of Jesus Christ that removes the affliction of devil spirits from people's lives. The evil spirits cannot stand in the presence of one who preaches Christ.

Acts 8:12

But when they believed Philip preaching the things concerning the kingdom of God, and the name of Jesus Christ, they were baptized, both men and women.

What did they believe in Samaria? They believed the things concerning the kingdom of God and the name of Jesus Christ.

In Acts 26, we find the record of Paul recounting to King Agrippa his conversion on the road to Damascus.

There is a remarkable truth in this record.

Acts 26:8-19

⁸ Why should it be thought a thing incredible with you, that God should raise the dead?

⁹ I verily thought with myself, that I ought to do many things contrary to the name of Jesus of Nazareth.

¹⁰ Which thing I also did in Jerusalem: and many of the saints did I shut up in prison, having received authority from the chief priests; and when they were put to death, I gave my voice against them.

¹¹ And I punished them oft in every synagogue, and compelled them to blaspheme; and being exceedingly mad against them, I persecuted them even unto strange cities.

¹² Whereupon as I went to Damascus with authority and commission from the chief priests,

¹³ At midday, O king, I saw in the way a light from heaven, above the brightness of the sun, shining round about me and them which journeyed with me.

¹⁴ And when we were all fallen to the earth, I heard a voice speaking unto me, and saying in the Hebrew tongue, Saul, Saul, why persecutest thou me? it is hard for thee to kick against the pricks.

¹⁵ And I said, Who art thou, Lord? And he said, I am Jesus whom thou persecutest.

¹⁶ But rise, and stand upon thy feet: for I have appeared unto thee for this purpose, to make thee a minister and a witness both of these things which thou hast seen, and of those things in the which I will appear unto thee;

¹⁷ Delivering thee from the people, and from the Gentiles, unto whom now I send thee,

¹⁸ To open their eyes, and to turn them from darkness to light, and from the power of Satan unto God, that they may receive forgiveness of sins, and inheritance among them which are sanctified by faith that is in me.

¹⁹ Whereupon, O king Agrippa, I was not disobedient unto the heavenly vision:

In verses 17 and 18, the Apostle Paul is given his purpose from his Lord, Jesus Christ. His purpose was to preach the Gospel that would open people's eyes and would turn people from darkness to light. The Gospel Paul preached would turn people from the power of Satan unto God, and they would receive forgiveness of sins and an inheritance, among those which are set apart by believing in Jesus Christ.

Today we are the ones to speak that which we have both seen and heard. There is a dying world out there that is lost with no direction and no leadership. We have the privilege today to speak the Words of life, which bring light and deliverance.

The Word of God spoken will open their eyes and turn them from darkness to light and from the power of Satan unto God. God's Word spoken on your lips will lead people to receive forgiveness of sins and an eternal inheritance!

Philippians 2:5-16

⁵ Let this mind be in you, which was also in Christ Jesus:

To be able to minister effectively in using the name of Jesus Christ, you must put on the mind of Christ.

⁶ Who, being in the form of God, thought it not robbery to be equal [agree] with God:

The word "form" means that Jesus was in an external appearance given to him by God. In his birth as a man, he received his form from God. God placed seed within Mary at our lord's conception.

The word "equal" means to agree with God. We can read in the Gospels where Jesus Christ stated that he always did the Father's will. He only did that which the Father showed him.

> [7] But made himself of no reputation, and took upon him the form of a servant, and was made in the likeness of men:
>
> [8] And being found in fashion as a man, he humbled himself, and became obedient unto death, even the death of the cross.
>
> [9] Wherefore God also hath highly exalted him, and given him a name which is above every name:
>
> [10] That at the name of Jesus every knee should bow, of things in heaven, and things in earth, and things under the earth;
>
> [11] And that every tongue should confess that Jesus Christ is Lord, to the glory of God the Father.
>
> [12] Wherefore, my beloved, as ye have always obeyed, not as in my presence only, but now much more in my absence, work out your own salvation with fear [respect] and trembling [obedience].
>
> [13] For it is God which worketh in you both to will and to do of his good pleasure.
>
> [14] Do all things without murmurings and disputings:

The things that we are to do without murmuring and disputing are the things which God works within us, both to will and to do of His good pleasure.

> [15] That ye may be blameless and harmless, the sons of God, without rebuke, in the midst of a crooked and perverse nation, among whom ye shine as lights in the world;
>
> [16] Holding forth the word of life; that I may rejoice in the day of Christ, that I have not run in vain, neither laboured in vain.

The name of Jesus Christ is the most powerful name I know. It is in his name that the sick are healed, the dead are raised to life, the sorrowful are made joyful. It is in his name that we receive eternal life.

Today, hold forth the Word of life in this most crooked and perverse world. The light of God's Word will dispel the darkness. The fleeting reward for the approval of men today pales in comparison to the eternal rewards in store for those obedient to God's calling.

Preach Jesus Christ everywhere you go. Shine as a light in this world holding forth the Word of Life!

Discussion Questions

1. Why is the name of Jesus Christ the most powerful name of all?

2. Share an example of when you used the name of Jesus Christ and you witnessed God's power in action.

3. When the first century apostles were told to stop speaking in the name of Jesus Christ what was their response? Have you ever been told to stop speaking the name of Jesus Christ and if so, what was your response?

4. Why was there great joy in Samaria?

5. In Acts 26 we see the Apostle Paul tell the story of his conversion. What is Paul's purpose as detailed in verse 18? What is your story of conversion? What do you see as your purpose as a child of God in this world?

CHAPTER 7

Our Hope – The Return of Jesus Christ

To know God and to know His wonderful son, our Lord and Savior Jesus Christ, is to joyfully anticipate his return. He will absolutely RETURN someday! It could be this afternoon, next week or 100 years from now. His return will happen in the fullness of times determined by God, and it will be an incredibly joyous moment! In our look at our hope, let's begin in the Book of Acts.

Acts 1:10, 11

[10] And while they looked stedfastly toward heaven as he went up, behold, two men stood by them in white apparel;

[11] Which also said, Ye men of Galilee, why stand ye gazing up into heaven? this same Jesus, which is taken up from you into heaven, shall so come in like manner as ye have seen him go into heaven.

Here we see the promise from God of the return of Jesus Christ. "This same Jesus," not some other Jesus, but this same Jesus shall absolutely return in the same manner that his disciples saw him taken up into heaven.

The Book of Acts is the pivot point between the Old Testament and the New Testament. The Gospels close out the Old Testament and complete the law. Everything that Jesus Christ did, he did to fulfill the law. In Romans 10:4, it states, "For Christ *is* the end of the law for righteousness to everyone that believeth."

In the New Testament, there are nine Church Epistles addressed specifically to the born-again believer. They are Romans, I and II Corinthians, Galatians, Ephesians, Philippians, Colossians and I and II Thessalonians. This is the *canonical order* (divinely appointed order) of these nine epistles, and the order never varies in the ancient Greek and Aramaic manuscripts.

I and II Thessalonians were the first epistles *chronologically* written to the born-again believer. Thessalonians was written first to give God's people a hope. Thessalonians goes into detail concerning the return of Jesus Christ. The heart of I and II Thessalonians deals with the return of Jesus Christ. God gave us the hope of the return of Jesus Christ to look forward to so that we can stand a lifetime for Him and His Word, no matter the pressures and persecutions of life. In our culture here in the United States, for the most part, the worst of the persecution will be a disparaging look or maybe some verbal ridicule. There are instances, though, where persecution is getting worse in this country with people losing jobs and incurring financial loss because of their beliefs.

In some parts of the world, it is a matter of life and death to stand for the truth of the one true God! At whichever

extreme it may be, with the hope of Jesus Christ's return burning in your heart, you will be able to stand and be bold and walk in love a lifetime, no matter what the persecution.

Joy is a result of
believing God's Word.

Let's begin to look at some of the great verses in this first chapter of I Thessalonians.

I Thessalonians 1:6

And ye became followers of us, and of the Lord, having received the word in much affliction, with joy of the Holy Ghost:

The believers in Thessalonica were followers, or imitators, of Paul, Silas and Timothy. It also says they were "followers of the Lord." The word "followers" is the Greek word *mimetes*, which means imitators. They were living the Word of God in their lives, which made them imitators of the lord.

The word "affliction" means pressures, specifically mental pressure. Despite the mental pressure that they endured, they received the Word of God with joy. They did not argue about the Word. They did not dismiss the Word as just another philosophy. It says, "they received it with joy."

Joy is a spiritual reality. Joy is inside your heart, regardless of the surrounding circumstances. It may be the darkest hour in your life, yet you can still have joy.

To see joy in all its greatness, look at the example of Jesus Christ in Hebrews.

Hebrews 12:2b

...who for the joy that was set before him endured the cross, despising the shame, and is set down at the right hand of the throne of God.

Jesus Christ endured excruciating pain, torture, and humiliation. Yet, he had joy!

The Thessalonian believers had joy even during intense pressure and persecution. Joy is much richer and deeper than happiness because happiness is dependent upon circumstances. Joy is a result of believing God's Word.

I Thessalonians 1:7

So that ye were ensamples to all that believe in Macedonia and Achaia.

The word "ensamples" is defined as a type an impress or a stamp; it is that which leaves a mark. The Thessalonian believers were speaking and living God's Word. They made an impact on those around them. They were examples, or a type, to all that believed in Macedonia and Achaia. Their believing, their boldness and their lives left an impact, or a mark, on their culture and society. When people encountered the believers from Thessalonica, they knew that the

Thessalonians had believed God's Word. They made a difference everywhere they went!

I Thessalonians 1:8

For from you sounded out the word of the Lord not only in Macedonia and Achaia, but also in every place your faith [believing] to God-ward is spread abroad; so that we need not to speak any thing.

What sounded out from the Thessalonian believers? The Word of the Lord! Not their opinions about the Word, not the current philosophy, not the socially acceptable politically correct speech, not the traditions of men - none of that! The Word of the Lord is what they spoke. They spoke God's Word!

If we as Christian believers today ever expect to see God's Word live mightily in our day and time, then we too must boldly speak God's Word and nothing but God's Word. We need to put our opinions and ego and pride behind us and move with the greatness of God's wonderful Word. We cannot hold onto the hurts, abuse or persecution from others in our lives. When we do, then the adversary has succeeded in neutralizing our lives for God. God is still the same God today as He was in the first century. He is still a God of miracles and deliverance when people believe His Word.

In Thessalonica, the believing of the born-again ones was spread throughout all the area. Paul did not have to comment on it; everybody knew it already.

I Thessalonians 1:9

For they themselves shew of us what manner of
entering in we had unto you, and how ye turned to
God from idols to serve the living and true God;

They turned to God from idols, and they served the living
and true God. Only God's Word can turn people from idols
to the living and true God. Idols are not just made of wood
or stone. Idols can be an image in a man's mind, in a woman's
mind. Those images can be our own ideologies or
philosophies that are contrary to God's Word. When our
social, political, or personal opinions and positions take
precedence over God's Word, then we have idols. Idols are
just as real today as they were 2,000 years ago. The people in
Thessalonica left their idols behind and turned to serve the
one true God.

Look what else they did in verse 10.

I Thessalonians 1:10

And to wait for his Son from heaven, whom he raised
from the dead, *even* Jesus, which delivered us from the
wrath to come.

They waited for the return of God's Son, Jesus Christ, from
heaven. The believers joyfully anticipated the return of their
Lord and Savior. When things sometimes got a little tough, or
they encountered persecution they did not turn back to their
old idols. They stayed put on God's Word. They could stand
fast during ridicule and persecution because they realized
their lives were meant for something greater than just today.

They knew that they had eternal life and that their full redemption would show itself at the return of Jesus Christ!

It also states in I Thessalonians 1:10 that "Jesus delivered us from the wrath to come." If we are delivered from the wrath to come, then we are delivered. Some believe that they will have to go through the whole tribulation period as described in the book of Revelation. Some others erroneously believe that halfway through the tribulation period is when Jesus Christ returns for the saints of God. Still others believe that we are rescued from the wrath to come and that Jesus Christ could return at any moment, then begins the tribulation period.

This talk about God's children having to go through the end times tribulation period and the wrath of God is not true. God loves His children, and His children have already been judged in Jesus Christ and declared righteous in God's sight. (See II Corinthians 5:21) God's Word says we have been delivered from the wrath to come. That settles it!

I Thessalonians 4:13-18

[13] But I would not have you to be ignorant, brethren, concerning them which are asleep, that ye sorrow not, even as others which have no hope.

[14] For if we believe that Jesus died and rose again, even so them also which sleep in Jesus will God bring with him.

[15] For this we say unto you by the word of the Lord, that we which are alive *and* remain unto the coming of

the Lord shall not prevent [precede or come before] them which are asleep.

[16] For the Lord himself shall descend from heaven with a shout, with the voice of the archangel, and with the trump of God: and the dead in Christ shall rise first:

[17] Then we which are alive *and* remain shall be caught up together with them in the clouds, to meet the Lord in the air: and so shall we ever be with the Lord.

[18] Wherefore comfort one another with these words.

We are patiently waiting for the return of our brother, Jesus Christ! As we wait, we joyfully speak and live God's Word, looking to the heavens, anticipating our full redemption in all its glory. Our hope comes into fruition when Jesus Christ, our Lord, returns from heaven. Then "the dead in Christ shall rise first: and we who are alive and remain shall be caught up together with them in the clouds, to meet the Lord in the air." The return of our Lord Jesus Christ from heaven is our hope!

Additional Thoughts

I Corinthians 15:51-58

[51] Behold, I shew you a mystery; We shall not all sleep, but we shall all be changed,

[52] In a moment, in the twinkling of an eye, at the last trump: for the trumpet shall sound, and the dead shall be raised incorruptible, and we shall be changed.

[53] For this corruptible must put on incorruption, and this mortal must put on immortality.

[54] So when this corruptible shall have put on incorruption, and this mortal shall have put on immortality, then shall be brought to pass the saying that is written, Death is swallowed up in victory.

[55] O death, where is thy sting? O grave, where is thy victory?

[56] The sting of death is sin; and the strength of sin is the law.

[57] But thanks be to God, which giveth us the victory through our Lord Jesus Christ.

[58] Therefore, my beloved brethren, be ye stedfast, unmoveable, always abounding in the work of the Lord, forasmuch as ye know that your labour is not in vain in the Lord.

The change that we will experience at the return of Jesus Christ will be a change of a very radical kind. The moment that this change occurs will be in an instant.

We are to be unmovable in our work for the Lord because we have the eternal victory through our Lord Jesus Christ!

If you were a research scientist and you discovered the cure to cancer – it never failed, no matter what type of cancer – you had the cure! Would you not give everyone the cure? Sure you would. You would talk about the cure everywhere, every day.

Well, we have so much more than a cure for cancer. We have the cure to death: the Lord Jesus Christ! He is the one that has redeemed mankind from the clutches of the evil one. He is the one that will one-day return, gathering his people together to live in a glorious eternity. Our labor is not in vain in the Lord! We have the cure! We have the answer, the antidote, the solution to all that ails mankind.

Colossians 1:12-14

[12] Giving thanks unto the Father, which hath made us meet [adequate or qualified] to be partakers of the inheritance of the saints in light:

[13] Who hath delivered us from the power of darkness, and hath translated us into the kingdom of his dear Son:

[14] In whom we have redemption through his blood, even the forgiveness of sins:

We are qualified to receive our inheritance because of the accomplished work of Jesus Christ. Our adequacy is not of our own works. We are partakers in the inheritance of the saints in light. The greatness and the fullness of our inheritance will be revealed at the return of Jesus Christ!

Ephesians 1:10-12

[10] That in the dispensation of the fulness of times he might gather together in one all things in Christ, both which are in heaven, and which are on earth; even in him:

[11] In whom also we have obtained an inheritance, being predestinated according to the purpose of him who worketh all things after the counsel of his own will:

[12] That we should be to the praise of his glory, who first trusted in Christ.

The gathering of God's children to meet the Lord in the air is the culmination of the fullness of times. Live today as if he could return at any moment! Your joy is found in living for your Lord!

Discussion Questions

1. How does the hope of Christ's return help you to stand for God today?

2. In what way are the Thessalonian believers an example to the church today?

3. The Thessalonian believers turned to God from their idols. Is there anything in your life that keeps you from God? How might you turn from those idols to God?

4. The great hope is the return of Jesus Christ. How should you live day-by-day as you anticipate Christ's return?

5. Your gathering together to meet the Lord in the air takes place at the fullness of times. What can you thank God for today as you wait for the return of Jesus Christ?

CHAPTER 8

Pray – Listen – Act

There are many records in the Bible where people pray to God. God hears their prayers, and God responds. Those that prayed then act according to God's response or direction. There are two tremendous examples of this in the book of Acts chapter 10.

Acts 10:1

There was a certain man in Caesarea called Cornelius, a centurion of the band called the Italian band,

Cornelius lived in Caesarea. He was a Roman soldier in a leadership position. He was a centurion in command of 100 men.

Acts 10:2

A devout man, and one that feared God with all his house, which gave much alms to the people, and prayed to God always.

Of even greater significance than being a leader in the Roman military, Cornelius was a devout man who reverenced God.

He shared of his abundance with the people of that area, and he was a man of prayer.

Acts 10:3-6

> [3] He saw in a vision evidently about the ninth hour of the day [3 pm] an angel of God coming in to him, and saying unto him, Cornelius.

> [4] And when he looked on him, he was afraid, and said, What is it, Lord? And he said unto him, Thy prayers and thine alms are come up for a memorial before God.

God heard his prayer! It does not say what Cornelius prayed, but based on the answer from God, which we see later in this chapter, his prayer had something to do with a desire to know God more intimately.

> [5] And now send men to Joppa, and call for one Simon, whose surname is Peter:

> [6] He lodgeth with one Simon a tanner, whose house is by the sea side: he shall tell thee what thou oughtest to do.

Joppa is about 30 miles southeast of Caesarea. That would be a two-day journey. The instruction from the angel is specific: "Find Peter from Joppa who lives with Simon a tanner whose house is by the sea."

When God gives instruction, either by way of an angel or revelation by the spirit, you do not need to guess. Your Heavenly Father will ensure that you have all that you need to know at that moment in time. As you are obedient to the instruction given then there may be additional information given from God as it is needed.

Acts 10:7-9

⁷ And when the angel which spake unto Cornelius was departed, he called two of his household servants, and a devout soldier of them that waited on him continually;

⁸ And when he had declared all these things unto them, he sent them to Joppa.

⁹ On the morrow, as they went on their journey, and drew nigh unto the city, Peter went up upon the housetop to pray about the sixth hour [around noon]:

In that culture, the housetop would be a quiet place to go to pray. The rooftops were flat, not steeped as our roofs are today.

As the servants from Cornelius approached Joppa, Peter went up to the housetop to pray.

Acts 10:10-16

¹⁰ And he [Peter] became *very hungry*, and would have eaten: but while they made ready, he fell into a trance,

The words "fell into a trance" is not a trance in our modern usage of that word. *Trance* would be better translated as amazement or astonishment. Peter was fully conscious and aware of what God was about to show him by revelation.

Peter came into great amazement by what he was seeing by revelation.

> [11] And saw heaven opened, and a certain vessel descending upon him, as it had been a great sheet knit at the four corners, and let down to the earth:
>
> [12] Wherein were all manner of fourfooted beasts of the earth, and wild beasts, and creeping things, and fowls of the air.
>
> [13] And there came a voice to him, Rise, Peter; kill, and eat. [He not only saw but he heard].
>
> [14] But Peter said, Not so, Lord; for I have never eaten any thing that is common or unclean. [Common or unclean would be defiled according to the Jewish law].
>
> [15] And the voice spake unto him again the second time, What God hath cleansed, that call not thou common.
>
> [16] This was done thrice: and the vessel was received up again into heaven.

Three times this happened.

Acts 10:17-22

> [17] Now while Peter doubted [questioned] in himself what this vision which he had seen should mean, behold, the men which were sent from Cornelius had made enquiry for Simon's house, and stood before the gate,

¹⁸ And called, and asked whether Simon, which was surnamed Peter, were lodged there.

¹⁹ While Peter thought on the vision, the Spirit said unto him, Behold, three men seek thee.

²⁰ Arise therefore, and get thee down, and go with them, doubting nothing: for I have sent them.

²¹ Then Peter went down to the men which were sent unto him from Cornelius; and said, Behold, I am he whom ye seek: what is the cause wherefore ye are come?

²² And they said, Cornelius the centurion, a just man, and one that feareth [reverences] God, and of good report among all the nation of the Jews, was warned [instructed] from God by an holy angel to send for thee into his house, and to hear words of thee.

In other words, God told Cornelius to send these men to Peter and to bring him back to Cornelius' house to hear what he has to say. What do you think Peter is going to talk about? The weather, the latest economic indicators? No. He is going to talk to the household of Cornelius about salvation through Jesus Christ!

Acts 10:23-33

²³ Then called he them in, and lodged them. And on the morrow Peter went away with them, and certain brethren from Joppa accompanied him.

Acts 11:12 tells us that there were six others who went with Peter. For Peter to go into the home of a Gentile is a big deal in that culture. It would not be right because he would be defiling himself according to the Jewish law. The Jews considered the Gentiles to be unclean. He took the others with him as support and witnesses.

²⁴ And the morrow after they entered into Caesarea. And Cornelius waited for them, and he had called together his kinsmen and near friends.

Cornelius was watching and waiting for them to arrive. He knew Peter would be coming.

²⁵ And as Peter was coming in, Cornelius met him, and fell down at his feet, and worshipped him.

²⁶ But Peter took him up, saying, Stand up; I myself also am a man.

²⁷ And as he talked with him, he went in, and found many that were come together.

Cornelius so confidently believed the message given from the angel sent by God that his house was filled with many anticipating the arrival of Peter and his message. Cornelius was a man of influence in the community. He was a leader. He was respected. Many took heed to the invite of Cornelius to come hear Peter speak.

²⁸ And he said unto them, Ye know how that it is an unlawful thing for a man that is a Jew to keep company, or come unto one of another nation; but God hath shewed me that I should not call any man common or unclean.

Remember the revelation Peter received while praying on the rooftop? Now it all fit together in his understanding. God did not consider the Gentiles to be unclean, and neither should Peter.

²⁹ Therefore came I unto you without gainsaying [arguing], as soon as I was sent for: I ask therefore for what intent ye have sent for me?

There are tremendous benefits and blessings to both Peter and Cornelius because of their obedience to do what God showed them.

Cornelius now restates his revelation before Peter and those present in his house.

³⁰ And Cornelius said, Four days ago I was fasting until this hour; and at the ninth hour I prayed in my house, and, behold, a man stood before me in bright clothing,

³¹ And said, Cornelius, thy prayer is heard, and thine alms are had in remembrance in the sight of God.

³² Send therefore to Joppa, and call hither Simon, whose surname is Peter; he is lodged in the house of

one Simon a tanner by the sea side: who, when he cometh, shall speak unto thee.

[33] Immediately therefore I sent to thee; and thou hast well done that thou art come. Now therefore are we all here present before God, to hear all things that are commanded thee of God.

There is significant importance to the word *immediately*. Cornelius did not wait. He did not sit and think about it, wondering if that was really God or just his imagination. Nor did he find an excuse of why not to do what the angel instructed.

Cornelius and his household wanted to know what God had to say. They desired to hear God's word from Peter, to hear that which was commanded of God for Peter to speak. There are still people throughout the world today that desire to hear what God has to say.

Acts 10:34

Then Peter opened his mouth, and said, Of a truth I perceive that God is no respecter of persons:

What a wonderful truth! God is no respecter of persons. Remember John 3:16, "For God so loved the world that He gave His only begotten son." God loves people. God's ministers are to love people and not to be respecters of persons. Peter recognized that God considers all people valuable in His sight.

Peter then states that which God instructs him to speak.

Acts 10:35-43

³⁵ But in every nation he that feareth him, and worketh righteousness, is accepted with him.

³⁶ The word which God sent unto the children of Israel, preaching peace by Jesus Christ: (he is Lord of all:)

³⁷ That word, I say, ye know, which was published throughout all Judaea, and began from Galilee, after the baptism which John preached;

³⁸ How God anointed Jesus of Nazareth with the Holy Ghost and with power: who went about doing good, and healing all that were oppressed of the devil; for God was with him.

³⁹ And we are witnesses of all things which he did both in the land of the Jews, and in Jerusalem; whom they slew and hanged on a tree:

⁴⁰ Him God raised up the third day, and shewed him openly;

⁴¹ Not to all the people, but unto witnesses chosen before God, even to us, who did eat and drink with him after he rose from the dead.

⁴² And he commanded us to preach unto the people, and to testify that it is he which was ordained of God to be the Judge of quick [living] and dead.

> [43] To him give all the prophets witness, that through his name whosoever believeth in him shall receive remission of sins.

Here, in these few short verses, Peter shares with all that are present how to become born again, how to receive the gift of holy spirit and become a son of God.

One must believe that God raised Jesus Christ from the dead and confess Jesus as Lord. That's it! There is nothing additional to do. Accept God's solution to man's predicament. Jesus Christ is the one and only way to the one true God!

Acts 10:44

> While Peter yet spake these words, the Holy Ghost fell on all them which heard the word.

The holy spirit fell on those who heard the words that Peter spoke. They believed the words that Peter spoke! They received the gift of holy spirit – eternal life!

Acts 10:45-46

> [45] And they of the circumcision which believed were astonished, as many as came with Peter, because that on the Gentiles also was poured out the gift of the Holy Ghost.

The six that came with Peter were astonished! The Gentiles received the new birth. The Gentiles were sons of God. The God of Israel was the God of all people!

How did they know that the household of Cornelius received the gift of holy spirit? Verse 46 tells us.

> [46] For they heard them speak with tongues, and magnify God.

They heard them speak in tongues, just as the twelve did on the day of Pentecost and just as all those that had believed from the Jewish religion up to that day. Speaking in tongues is the indisputable proof in the senses realm that one has received the gift of holy spirit. Speaking in tongues is what convinced the six that came with Peter that the holy spirit had been poured out upon Gentiles.

Not only were those six astonished, that day had spiritual reverberations that will last through all eternity! When the angels in heaven saw the gift of God poured out on the Gentiles, they rejoiced with great rejoicing. The angels marveled at the manifold wisdom of God.

Pray – Listen – Act

Furthermore, on the evil side, the devil and his minions cringed in horror to see that God's grace and gift of eternal life were available for all mankind, to all that would believe on the Lord Jesus Christ!

Here in Acts 10, we have two remarkable examples of prayer to God by Peter and Cornelius. God answered their prayers by giving them direction, and both Peter and Cornelius were obedient to God's instruction.

What joy and rejoicing in the life of Peter and the six that came with him! What joy and rejoicing in the life of Cornelius and those that were with him!

God is no respecter of persons. God hears your prayer. Anticipate your answer from God. Be obedient to His instruction. Rejoice with boundless joy!

Additional Thoughts

Ephesians 6:18

Praying always with all prayer and supplication in the Spirit, and watching thereunto with all perseverance and supplication for all saints;

We are encouraged to pray always with all prayer and supplication in the spirit. To pray in the spirit, or by way of the spirit, is to speak in tongues. In Acts 10, it says that when they spoke in tongues, they magnified God. Speaking in tongues is also prayer in the spirit. We are to pray for one another and to watch over one another with all perseverance. We make requests to God for one another. One of the ways that we do this is to speak in tongues.

Romans 12:12

Rejoicing in hope; patient in tribulation; continuing instant in prayer;

We are to be instant in prayer. The word "instant" means to be quick to pray and always ready to pray. Prayer is to be our way of life. We are to pray with our understanding and pray in the spirit.

I Thessalonians 5:16-19

[16] Rejoice evermore.

[17] Pray without ceasing.

[18] In every thing give thanks: for this is the will of God in Christ Jesus concerning you.

[19] Quench not the Spirit.

Rejoice in all the Father has done for you. Let prayer permeate your every breath, giving thanks to God. Go to your Heavenly Father with great expectation in prayer. Anticipate an answer and then whatever He shows you, obediently act.

Discussion Questions

1. Cornelius was a Gentile. Did God answer his prayer? Was Cornelius obedient to the instruction from the angel? In your prayer life, have you seen a time when your answer from God contained instructions for you to carry out to see the answer come into fruition?

2. Look up Ephesians 3:20. How might this verse give you direction in your prayer life?

3. What did Peter talk about when he arrived at Cornelius' house?

4. How did Peter and the six that came with him know that Cornelius and his household believed the words that Peter spoke?

5. What verses of scripture have had an impact on your prayer life? Why?

CHAPTER 9

Heart's Desire – To Know the Living Christ

A re you sidetracked by the flesh? Does the flesh keep you from knowing who you are in Christ? Have we relegated the work of God to that of nothing more than a safety net – having received eternal life?

In Philippians chapter three, we see the Apostle Paul, who according to the standards of the flesh, in the eyes of the world, had it all.

Philippians 3:4-9

⁴ Though I might also have confidence in the flesh. If any other man thinketh that he hath whereof he might trust in the flesh, I more:

Here, Paul is literally saying, "Look, you think you have your life together in the flesh? Well, I have you beat. Look at what my life was in the flesh!"

Then in verse five he begins to tell us about his life in the flesh.

> [5] Circumcised the eighth day, of the stock of Israel, of the tribe of Benjamin, an Hebrew of the Hebrews; as touching the law, a Pharisee;

Paul was a full-blooded Jew. He had all the right heritage, and it could be traced back to the tribe of Benjamin. His life mattered in the eyes of the world because of what side of the tracks he came from.

> [6] Concerning zeal, persecuting the church; touching the righteousness which is in the law, blameless.

Philippians 3:6 (Phillips translation)

As far as keeping the Law is concerned I was a Pharisee, and you can judge my enthusiasm for the Jewish faith by my active persecution of the Church. *As far as the Law's righteousness is concerned, I don't think anyone could have found fault with me.*

If one were to consider the life of Paul, no fault would be found in his flesh! He did all the right things at all the right times. He said all the right words when they needed to be said. He was the kind of guy who if you got to hang out with him, you would make sure your neighbors and co-workers knew.

> [7] But what things were gain to me, those I counted loss for Christ.

> [8] Yea doubtless, and I count all things but loss for the excellency of the knowledge of Christ Jesus my Lord: for whom I have suffered the loss of all things, and do count them but dung, that I may win Christ,

All the worldly prestige, all the privilege, all the accolades of men were nothing but dung to Paul in light of gaining Christ and knowing Christ Jesus as his Lord!

> [9] And be found in him, not having mine own righteousness, which is of the law, but that which is through the faith of Christ, the righteousness which is of God by faith:

Philippians 3:9 (Phillips translation)

> For now my place is in him, and I am not dependent upon any of the self-achieved righteousness of the Law. God has given me that genuine righteousness which comes from faith in Christ. *How changed are my ambitions!* Now I long to know Christ and the power shown by his resurrection.

Paul's ambitions, desires and motivations changed. The prestige, the worldly acclaim that most strive for, no longer had any hold on Paul. He recognized his calling in Christ. He saw his life through the eyes of his Heavenly Father. The value of your life is identical to the value of Paul's life in the eyes of God! Your life is even equal in value to our Father as the life of the Lord Jesus Christ! Paul's heart was illuminated by the righteousness which comes from believing in Christ.

Philippians 3:12-14 (Phillips translation)

Yet, my brothers, I do not consider myself to have "arrived", spiritually, nor do I consider myself already perfect. But I keep going on, grasping ever more firmly that purpose for which Christ grasped me. My brothers, I do not consider myself to have fully grasped it even now. But I do concentrate on this: I leave the past behind and with hands outstretched to whatever lies ahead I go straight for the goal—my reward the honour of being called by God in Christ.

The King James version of verses 13 and 14 states, "...forgetting those things which are behind, and reaching forth unto those things which are before, I press toward [I exert effort toward] the mark for the prize of the high calling of God in Christ Jesus."

Forget those things which are behind. Yesterday is gone. Forget the rewards of the world and pursue after the reward of God's high calling in Christ!

Here in Philippians chapter three, we see Paul not allowing the distractions and deceitfulness of the rewards of the world to keep him from knowing who he is in Christ.

I must ask you a question. I ask it of myself as well. Do you believe God? Do I believe God? Or do we just mentally assent to His Word.

Mental assent is to say what God says, but never literally *act* upon His Word. You and I may have a tremendous knowledge of God and His Word. We may know all *about* God. But do we know God?

- Do you desire to know God as Abraham knew God? God called Abraham His friend.

- Do you desire to know God as Moses knew God? God said He knew Moses face to face.

- Do you desire to know God as David knew God? God said David was a man after God's own heart.

- Do you desire to know God as your Heavenly Father, as Jesus Christ knew God as his Heavenly Father? God said Jesus was His beloved son in whom He was well pleased.

Today is your day to know God!

Yesterday is gone. Tomorrow may never arrive. This moment, right now, you have been called to forget the past and to press toward the mark for the prize of the high calling in Christ Jesus!

The Word of God is true. It is not a collection of remarkable stories, nor is it the philosophies and ideas of men. The Bible is God's communication to those He loves.

Ephesians 1:3

Blessed be the God and Father of our Lord Jesus Christ, who hath blessed us with all spiritual blessings in heavenly places in Christ:

Ephesians 1:3 (Phillips translation)

Praise be to God for giving us through Christ every possible spiritual benefit as citizens of Heaven!"

Philippians 3:20

For our conversation [citizenship] is in heaven; from whence also we look for the Saviour, the Lord Jesus Christ:

In this world, we may live in the United States or Canada or Ireland or Russia or Africa. This world will pass away someday. We are citizens of heaven. Our heavenly citizenship transcends and supersedes our earthly citizenship. The heart of our true calling in our heavenly citizenship looks to heaven for our soon returning savior, the Lord Jesus Christ!

Ephesians 1:6

To the praise of the glory of his grace, wherein he hath made us [you – insert your name!] accepted in the beloved.

You are accepted. Oh, how people today try so hard to be accepted of others. Quit trying! You are accepted in the beloved. Remember Paul in Philippians three. In his flesh he was accepted by his peers, but he considered it all dung in comparison to his acceptance in Christ. Your Heavenly Father has made you accepted according to His standards. He has clothed you in a righteousness which fades not away!

Colossians 1:12

Giving thanks unto the Father, which hath made us meet [or adequate] to be partakers of the inheritance of the saints in light:

God has fully equipped you to partake in the inheritance that He has made available. It is an inheritance to be enjoyed through all eternity! This 60, 70, 80, 90 years that we may have here on earth is not all there is! There is an entire eternity available for God's children that will go on forever and ever. It will begin on that great and glorious day when the Lord Jesus Christ RETURNS!

Until the moment of his return, we have a life here to live for Him. So many are looking for a purpose in life. Many want to lead a fulfilling life, a life that has meaning. Some may ask, "What am I supposed to do?" It is a good question. It is a question whose answer is found in God's Word.

II Corinthians 5:14, 15

[14] For the love of Christ constraineth us [the love of Christ works and urges our hearts to live for him]; because we thus judge, that if one died for all, then were all dead:

[15] And that he died for all, that they which live should not henceforth live unto themselves, but unto him which died for them, and rose again.

There is your purpose! You are to no longer live for your own desires and the pleasures of the world, rather live for

Christ. We serve God. God doesn't serve us. God is not our errand boy doing as we dictate in our prayer life.

Take the time to look at all the prayers prayed in the book of Acts and the Church Epistles sometime. It may surprise you

as to what they prayed for compared to what we so often pray for in our prayer meetings. The prayers in Acts and Romans through Thessalonians are examples of the prayers that we are to pray today.

God has already given you all there is to give in Christ.

God has already given you all there is to give in Christ. In Colossians 2:10, it says that you are complete in Christ. It literally says that you are completely, completely, absolutely complete in him. If you are that complete are you lacking anything?

You have all authority to use the name of Jesus Christ. That name is above every name. Everything in heaven and on earth bows to the name of Jesus! Walk into and live who you are in Christ! Utilize the power and authority that has been given to you.

Colossians 3:1-4

¹ If ye then be risen with Christ, seek those things which are above, where Christ sitteth on the right hand of God.

² Set your affection [your thoughts] on things above, not on things on the earth.

³ For ye are dead, and your life is hid with Christ in God.

⁴ When Christ, who is our life, shall appear, then shall ye also appear with him in glory.

Your real life is hidden with Christ in God. If you want to know who you really are, get to know the living Christ within. How do you begin to know the living Christ within? There are three ways to get to know the living Christ within:

1. Read the gospels to see how Jesus Christ loved God and people. Look at his example of obedience to do as his Heavenly Father directed.

2. Read the church epistles (Romans through Thessalonians) to know what God has made you to be in Christ.

When it comes to reading the church epistles, it is not enough for you to just casually read in between checking emails and replying to text messages. Allow the Word to become living and real to you by believing what you read. When you believe the written Word, you will live the written Word. Think God's Word. Speak God's Word. Live God's Word. Allow your heart to marinate in God's Word.

It is so much more than just setting aside 20 or 30 minutes per day. It is not a method in the sense of fulfilling a duty and "putting in the time." It is heart. Surely it involves setting time aside each day, but it is not a rush to read through a chapter or a book. You may spend 20 minutes on one verse of scripture, thinking about it and asking God to open your eyes to the depth of the truth contained in that scripture. Read the verse in various translations. Think about what you have read throughout the day.

3. Operate the manifestations of holy spirit in your day-to-day life. There are nine manifestations listed in I Corinthians 12:7-11. The manifestations are speaking in tongues, interpretation of tongues, prophecy, word of knowledge, word of wisdom, discerning of spirits, believing, miracles and healing.

The manifestations are the evidence of the gift of holy spirit which you received at the time of the new birth. When you believed that God raised Jesus Christ from the dead and confessed Jesus as Lord you received Christ within you. The Christ within gives you the ability to operate the manifestations of holy spirit.

It is in the operation of the manifestations of holy spirit and knowing who you are in Christ that you will clearly see the great and high calling God has called you to! I can assure you that you will never have a boring day in your life when your identity in Christ becomes living and real to you. I have had glimpses of it, and I want more!

Humbly but confidently go to your Heavenly Father and ask Him to open the eyes of your understanding as you read His Word. He will! Ask Him to teach you to know the Christ within. He will!

God will open the eyes of your understanding. He will teach you how He works within you.

Philippians 2:13

For it is God which worketh in you both to will and to do of his good pleasure.

Place your own name into this verse. It is God who works within you Mike, Alanna, Josiah, and Carmen! It is God who works within YOU!

Ephesians 2:10

For we are his workmanship, created in Christ Jesus unto good works, which God hath before ordained [prepared] that we should walk in them.

You are God's workmanship, created in Christ Jesus. You are a three part being: body, soul and spirit. Which of those three is created? The spirit is created. The body is formed, and the soul is made. You are His workmanship, created in Christ Jesus unto good works. The good works that God has prepared beforehand for you are works of the spirit. It is that Christ within which allows you to operate the manifestations of holy spirit. Signs, miracles and wonders - those are the good works that God has called you to.

Believe that God is who He says He is. Believe that you are who God says you are. To believe is to live accordingly. To believe is to take heed to God's working within your heart and life and then to carry out what He has requested of you. The Creator of the heavens and the earth talks to His children. He talks to you. He makes known His ways and His heart to those that are willing to listen and believe.

Let your heart's desire be to know the living Christ within!

Additional Thoughts

The prayers contained in the church epistles are the prayers that we can pray. Considering that we know the Christ within, let's look at Ephesians chapter 1.

Ephesians 1:16-19

¹⁶ Cease not to give thanks for you, making mention of you in my prayers;

Paul prayed for the believers. In the next verses, we see specifically what he prayed for.

¹⁷ That the God of our Lord Jesus Christ, the Father of glory, may give unto you the spirit of wisdom and revelation in the knowledge of him:

¹⁸ The eyes of your understanding [heart] being enlightened; that ye may know what is the hope of his calling, and what the riches of the glory of his [God's] inheritance in the saints,

¹⁹ And what is the exceeding greatness of his power to us-ward who believe, according to the working of his mighty power

God desires for us to know three truths:

1. What the hope of His calling is.

2. What is God's inheritance. God's inheritance is His people. You are what God gets out of this deal and He is well pleased that you are His!

3. What is the exceeding greatness of His power which you have received and is available to operate when you believe.

What an awesome privilege to live for Him. You are blessed. No one was missed with His goodness. His love and care and concern and grace and mercy are never ending. God has blessed you through His son, the Lord Jesus Christ.

Discussion Questions

1. How did Paul's earthly qualifications measure up against who he was in Christ?

2. Do you see yourself more as who you are in Christ or as who you are based on the world's standard? Why?

3. Today is your day to grow in your relationship with God as your Heavenly Father. List three verses that help you to recognize God's love and care for you.

4. What are the three ways listed in this chapter to help you to know who you are in Christ?

5. In Ephesians 2:10 you see that you are God's workmanship created in Christ Jesus to do the works that God has prepared for you. What is God working in your heart and life to do for Him?

CHAPTER 10

A Matter of the Heart

The accomplished work of Jesus Christ includes: his death, his resurrection from the dead, his ascension into heaven, and his sending of the gift of holy spirit on the day of Pentecost. Your salvation is complete. There is no additional work on your part to be accepted by God. Jesus Christ is your righteousness.

Now through God's grace, mercy and love – which is demonstrated in the accomplished work of Jesus Christ – you are able to live above the circumstances of the world, making known the living Christ to a dying world.

Now, how do we live the spiritually victorious life that is available to us today?

We will begin in the Old Testament. Here the foundation will be laid for us to live as God intended. The Old Testament is for our learning. It is not addressed to us today. The Old Testament is addressed to the children of Israel, though we can surely learn great truth from the Old Testament scriptures.

An example that clearly illustrates this truth: suppose you received a letter through the mail from a dear friend. The letter is addressed to you. It is TO you. You allow me to read the letter. The letter is not addressed to me, though I can learn something from its contents. So is the Old Testament for us today.

Romans 15:4

For whatsoever things were written aforetime [before the day of Pentecost] were written for our learning, that we through patience and comfort of the scriptures might have hope.

Romans 15:4 (Phillips Translation)

For all those words which were written long ago are meant to teach us today; that when we read in the scriptures of the endurance of men and of all the help that God gave them in those days, we may be encouraged to go on hoping in our own time.

When we see in the Old Testament God's clear instruction and His mighty hand of deliverance for His people, it encourages us today. It helps us to stand strong.

In Proverbs chapter four, we see part of what is needed to live a victorious life today with and for God.

Proverbs 4:20-23

[20] My son, attend [pay attention or take heed to] to my words; incline thine ear unto my sayings [hear the Word of God].

> [21] Let them [God's Words] not depart from thine eyes;
> keep them [God's Words] in the midst of thine heart.

We keep the Word of God in our hearts by not letting the Word depart from our eyes. It is not just our physical eyes, it is the eye of the mind. Meditate on the Word that you have read and heard.

> [22] For they [God's Words] are life unto those that find them, and health to all their flesh.

God's Word is life. Jesus Christ stated in the Gospel of John 6:63, "the words that I speak unto you are spirit and they are life." In Hebrews 4:12 it states, "the Word of God is quick and powerful." It is a living and energizing Word. God's Word is alive. It is life and health.

> [23] Keep thy heart with all diligence; for out of it [the heart] are the issues of life.

Keep your heart. What is it to *keep your heart?* To "keep" is to guard or to be a watchman over. Guard your heart with all diligence. "With all diligence" is to keep your heart above all that is kept, above all that is worth keeping. It must be very important for us to guard our hearts if God's Word directs us to be watchmen over our hearts above all else that we may watch over!

How do we guard our hearts? One thought at a time, that is how we guard our hearts. Some might say, "How can I do that? My mind is so scattered." Start right here, right now! Change your thinking; think, "I control my mind to think the things of God, to think on His Word!"

Why?

> [23] ...for out of it [out of the heart – the heart being
> the innermost part of the mind; the heart is that
> which makes you, you. It is the seat of your personal
> life, it is where your life emanates from] are the issues
> of life.

The issues of your life come from your heart. "Issues" could
be translated as source. The *source* of your life comes from
your heart. Source is believing. What you believe is what you
do! What you believe determines who you are!

Now, one could have the spirit of God and never live as if he
or she had the spirit. One could be a child of God and live a
life of total defeat. What a sad situation!

How could that happen? It could happen because of not
guarding the heart, of not being a watchman over the
thoughts one thinks and dwells upon.

It is important to recognize here that we are not talking about
the circumstances that may surround you. Circumstances do
not define whether you are defeated or victorious in life. With
a joyful heart, because of the Word of God in your thinking
and in your heart, you can live triumphantly in the
circumstances.

Would you allow a stranger to come to your house and dump
a garbage can of rotten, smelly waste on your living room
floor? No – of course not! Well, so often we allow that to
happen in our minds. We allow the world to dump its

garbage in our minds through the TV shows we watch, the music we listen to or the things we read.

Maybe you have never been taught how important it is to control your thinking – to be aware of what you allow your mind to dwell upon.

Here in Proverbs, we can see it is a matter of living life as God intended or being controlled by influences that are in direct opposition to God.

Would you like to live for God? Would you like to see a dramatic change in your life?

Psalm 119 contains a tremendous key in living with and for God.

Psalm 119:11

Thy word have I hid in mine heart, that I might not sin against thee.

Hide God's Word in your heart. Meditate on the Word of God. Think about His goodness and love! Hide His Word in your heart by controlling your mind to think God's Word.

Now, I think I need to clarify that we are not doing this to earn salvation or earn points with God. Jesus Christ already earned salvation for all. Once you have confessed Jesus as Lord and believed God raised him from the dead, you have eternal life. Your "points with God" are wrapped up in your righteousness and your sanctification in Christ. You already have all the points you will ever receive. You have received all spiritual blessings in heavenly places, and you are accepted in the beloved.

We hide God's Word in our heart and keep our hearts with all diligence because we love God. It is a privilege and joy to live victoriously in this life carrying out the works that God has prepared for us to do!

Here are a couple more verses in the Old Testament about controlling our thinking and the benefits of doing so.

Isaiah 26:3

Thou [God] wilt keep him [you] in perfect peace, whose mind is stayed [or fixed] on thee [God]: because he [you] trust in thee [God].

In that verse, we see that both God and you have a responsibility. Your responsibility is to fix your mind on God. To fix your mind on God is to think about God and His Word. Think about His goodness, His love. God's responsibility is to keep you in perfect peace. The peace that comes from God far surpasses the peace you might try to generate by your own devices.

We live in a very un-peaceful world. Without God, people are anxious, worried and fearful. What do people do for a make-believe peace when they do not know God? They sedate themselves with pharmaceuticals, they drink alcohol to numb the pain, they take drugs to escape the circumstance, or they immerse themselves in an activity to avoid the pain and heartache of a life without God. For many, that has become the norm. Living like that is not normal! It does not have to be that way. Believe me, I know what I'm talking about. I have been there before. When I came back to God, He was there with His loving arms wide open to comfort me and to give me His peace.

God gives you a peaceful heart when you trust Him!

Proverbs 3:1-3

¹My son, forget not my law [teaching]; but let thine heart keep my commandments [my Word]:

²For length of days, and long life, and peace, shall they add to thee.

Can any man of his own will add to his life length of days, a long life or peace? No, but God will add those to one's life whose heart contains His Word.

³Let not mercy and truth forsake thee: bind them about thy neck; write them upon the table of thine heart:

We are to write God's Word upon the table of our heart. Our heart is a slate upon which we write God's Word. We decide by the freedom of our will what thoughts we will entertain and hold onto in our minds. The words that we dwell on in our thinking determine the direction of our heart.

God said of David "he was a man after God's own heart!" David wrote many of the Psalms. When you read the Psalms that David wrote, notice how often he spoke of meditating on God's Word. He writes that he thought on God's Word throughout the day and night. David determined to have his heart become one with God's heart. He loved God. He loved God's Word.

You can also decide to have your heart become one with God's heart, just as David did.

Proverbs 3:4, 5

[4] So shalt thou find favour and good understanding in the sight of God and man.

[5] Trust in the Lord with all thine heart; and lean not unto thine own understanding.

When you trust God, you will never be disappointed. When you trust God, there is no worry or fear. When you have worry and fear, where do they reside? They live in your mind, in your heart. Where there is worry and fear, there is no peace. A heart without peace is painful.

Write God's will for your life upon the table of your heart by thinking and meditating on God's Word. Leave no room on the table of your heart for worry and fear. The light of God's Word dispels the darkness.

Look at the second half of verse five, "lean not unto your own understanding." Your own understanding is the way of the world. It is that which seems right to a man. It is unstable. It is faulty. It is a lie. When we lean on our own understanding, our life will collapse. We will fall.

Proverbs 3:6

> ⁶ In all thy ways acknowledge him, and he shall direct thy paths.

Acknowledge God by looking to Him and asking Him for the direction needed. He will help you. He will work within you to will and to do of His good pleasure. He will make straight your path. The light of His understanding and His wisdom will make clear to you the way you should go and what you should do. Man's wisdom is darkness. God's Word is a lamp for our feet and a light upon our path.

How do we live the spiritually victorious life that is available and made known in the scriptures?

Romans 12:1, 2

> ¹ I beseech you therefore, brethren, by the mercies of God, that ye present your bodies a living sacrifice, holy, acceptable unto God, which is your reasonable [logical] service.

Here we are lovingly implored to present ourselves as a living sacrifice, obedient to the calling of God. It is the only logical thing to do! The next verse will show us HOW to do just that.

> ² And be not conformed [molded or fashioned] to this world:…

What is it to be *conformed* to this world? To be conformed, molded, or fashioned to this world is to think and live according to the wisdom of this world. This world is in direct opposition to God.

For instance, to believe that you can get to the one true God without Jesus Christ is to be molded to this world. To think that by your good works, you can stand approved before God and receive eternal life is to be molded to this world. To believe that God makes people sick as punishment and that He kills people, is to be molded to this world.

There are many moral standards in our culture today that are contrary to the truth of God's Word.

Most people do not even know that they are controlled and conformed to this world. Their minds are fashioned by the TV and movies they watch, by the music they listen to, by the material they read. The words, ideas and images presented by the world are written on the heart of unsuspecting souls.

Romans 12:2b

... but [in contrast to being molded by the world] be ye transformed by the renewing of your mind, that ye may prove what is that good, and acceptable, and perfect, will of God.

To be *transformed* is to be transfigured. It is a change of a very radical kind. The word "transformed" in the Greek text is the word from which we get the English word *metamorphosis*. If you remember from your high school biology class, metamorphosis is the process that a caterpillar goes through when it enters the cocoon and comes out a beautiful butterfly.

Just as the lowly caterpillar is transformed into a lovely butterfly, so we, too, are transformed from the molding of this world to a loving, powerful son of God.

How are you transformed? You are transformed by the renewing of your mind. Put God's Word on in your thinking to the end that your heart is changed. Remember, the Word of God is a living Word. It is not a dead word. It is living. It is powerful. It is energizing. It is alive!

You have the responsibility to renew your mind. The *living* Word of God will bring about the transformation. When you combine the living Word of God in the heart of a man or woman along with the spirit of God within that individual, then you have a true transformation.

God will never take over your freedom of will. God does not control your thinking nor your actions.

When you received holy spirit at the new birth, you received all that God has to give spiritually in order for you to live a life that is like the life that Jesus Christ lived when he walked on the earth. To live that life practically day-by-day, you must become transformed by the renewing of your mind!

Philippians 2:5

Let this mind be in you, which was also in Christ Jesus:

The word "mind" is thoughts. Think the thoughts that Christ Jesus would think. To do that you must read the Word of God and hold that Word in your mind.

Ephesians 4:24

And that ye put on the new man, which after God is created in righteousness and true holiness.

What is the new man? The new man is the Christ within. You are to put the new man on in your thinking. Think what the Word says.

Colossians 3:1

If [Since] ye then be risen with Christ, seek [diligently pursue after] those things which are above, where Christ sitteth on the right hand of God.

What are the things that are above? There are many, but just to name a few:

- That your heart would be enlightened to the end that you would know the hope of His calling. (Ephesians 1:18)

- That you would know the riches of the glory of God's inheritance in you. (Ephesians 1:18)

- That you would know by experience the exceeding greatness of His power that is available to you when you believe. (Ephesians 1:19)

- That you would make full proof of the ministry which you have been called to. (II Timothy 4:5)

Those are wonderful truths "which are above" that you could diligently pursue after.

Colossians 3:2, 3

² Set your affection [your thoughts] on things above, not on things on the earth.

³ For ye are dead, and your life is hid with Christ in God.

In our identification in the accomplished work of Jesus Christ, we died with him. Our life is now hidden with Christ in God. Our life is concealed in Christ. As you come to know the living Christ within, by seeking those things which are above, you will live the supernatural life you are intended to live!

Colossians 3:4

When Christ, who is our life, shall appear, then shall ye also appear with him in glory.

The Lord Jesus Christ shall absolutely return in the fullness of time. At that moment, you shall absolutely appear with him in glory. What a motivation to seek those things which are above! What a wonderful hope we have!

Colossians 3:10

And have put on the new man, which is renewed in knowledge after the image of him that created him:

The new man is put on in your mind by your thinking. Have you ever felt like you needed a fresh start in life? Here is your fresh start today, right now! Put on the new man. Think the thoughts of who you are in Christ. You control your mind. You decide what you will think about. Put on the new man!

Colossians 3:12-15

[12] Put on therefore, as the elect of God, holy and beloved, bowels of mercies, kindness, humbleness of mind, meekness, longsuffering;

[13] Forbearing one another, and forgiving one another, if any man have a quarrel against any: even as Christ forgave you, so also do ye.

There is our standard for forgiveness. Even as Christ has forgiven you, you also forgive others.

[14] And above all these things put on charity, which is the bond of perfectness.

We are to put on charity. *Charity* is God's love. We are to put on the love of God in the renewed mind.

[15] And let the peace of God rule in your hearts, to the which also ye are called in one body; and be ye thankful.

As we put on the mind of Christ, we allow the peace of God to rule in our hearts.

II Corinthians 10:3-4

[3] For though we walk in the flesh, we do not war after the flesh:

[4] (For the weapons of our warfare are not carnal, but mighty through God to the pulling down of strong holds;)

The new man is put on in your mind by your thinking.

We live in this world, but our battle is not a battle with flesh.

There is a spiritual force behind the scenes that pulls strings. The ways of the world are in opposition to the purposes of God.

The battlefield is the mind. The weapons of warfare are words. The strongholds that need to be pulled down or removed are ideas, opinions, thoughts, doctrines, and schemes that are contrary to God's Word.

Do you conform to this world or are you transformed by the renewing of your mind?

II Corinthians 10:5

Casting down imaginations [human logic and reasoning], and every high [false] thing that exalts itself against the knowledge of God [or lifts itself above the knowledge of God], and bringing into captivity every thought to the obedience of Christ;

In other words, do not let your mind run wild. You decide what you will think about. When your thinking is in opposition to God, throw the thought out and replace it with the truth.

A mind that is *uncontrolled* is anxious, fearful, and defeated. A mind *controlled* is peaceful, loving, and victorious.

Remember we read earlier in Proverbs four that all the issues of life come from your heart. You are to direct your heart by the thoughts that you think. Believing God emanates from your heart.

Look again at Romans chapter 12.

Romans 12:2

And be not conformed to this world: but be ye transformed by the renewing of your mind, that ye may prove what is that good, and acceptable, and perfect, will of God.

Romans 12:2 (Phillips translation)

Don't let the world around you squeeze you into its mold, but let God re-mold your minds from within, so that you may prove in practice that the plan of God for you is good, meets all his demands and moves towards the goal of true maturity.

The Word of God is living. It is alive! It produces in your life what God intends when it lives within your heart. In Isaiah, God states that His Word accomplishes that which He pleases, and it prospers where it is sent.

We live our lives every moment of every day by words – words we think and believe.

The Creator of the heavens and the earth, the One in whom there is no darkness, has graciously given us His Word that we may be transformed by the renewing of our minds.

Go forth today and prove what is that good, acceptable, and perfect will of God!

Discussion Questions

1. Who is the Old Testament addressed to? What can you learn from the Old Testament?

2. What are you to guard with all diligence? Why?

3. How do you guard your heart?

4. What does it mean to renew your mind?

5. Colossians instructs us to set our thoughts on things above. What are some of those things above that you are to set your mind on?

CHAPTER 11

Complete in Christ

Have you ever felt empty inside? Almost as if there is a vacuum that needs to be filled? Have you ever thought that your life did not have much to offer? Many people, at one time or another, have thought of themselves in this way.

Many try to fill that emptiness with some type of addiction. It could be an addiction to drugs or alcohol. It could be an addiction to working 60 or more hours a week or immersing yourself in the lives of imaginary TV characters night after night. All those distractions are just that – a distraction. They are a poor substitute for what the heart of men and women truly long for.

The heart longs for a relationship with God. The heart yearns to be accepted and loved. The heart of a man or a woman desires to know that they are whole and that his or her life really does matter. It is only through the work of Jesus Christ that we find wholeness and meaning to life.

Colossians 2:9, 10

[9] For in him [Christ] dwelleth all the fulness of the Godhead bodily.

[10] And ye are complete in him, which is the head of all principality and power:

To be complete is nothing wanting, filled to full measure. If we are complete in Christ, then we are truly complete. It is the spirit of God within an individual that fills the emptiness in the heart and life of a man or a woman. When we see ourselves as inadequate or unworthy, we will lack the confidence and boldness to live the life God intended.

To manifest our completeness in Christ and to be more than conquerors, we must confess the Word of God and act as the Word of God directs. When we fail to confess and act as God's Word directs, then we fail to manifest the more than abundant life that Jesus Christ made available. When we do not believe God's Word, then we show forth less in our lives than that which rightfully belongs to us as sons of God.

This word "complete" in verse ten is an incredibly unique word in the original text. Literally, this verse says, "We are completely, completely, absolutely complete in him!" Such completeness is hard to comprehend. Surely, we can know for a certainty that we are lacking in nothing. If God's Word declares that we are complete in Christ, then we are complete in Christ!

Let's look at some other verses that indicate that we are complete.

Romans 3:24

Being justified freely by his grace through the
redemption that is in Christ Jesus:

The justification that you have received from God is the legal
acquittal from the guilt of sin. It is the absolute declaration
that you are righteous in God's sight. Jesus Christ redeemed
you from your sins. He paid the price. You have been
justified freely by God's grace.

What work could you do to earn justification? None! Jesus
Christ completed the perfect work. By God's grace, you have
been freely justified. Justification is simply "just as if you've
never sinned." God sees his children in Christ as He sees His
son, the Lord Jesus Christ! What a joy! What a time to be
alive and live with God, the Creator of the universe as your
Heavenly Father!

Romans 5:6-10

⁶ For when we were yet without strength, in due time
Christ died for the ungodly.

⁷ For scarcely for a righteous man will one die: yet
peradventure for a good man some would even dare
to die.

⁸ But God commendeth his love toward us, in that,
while we were yet sinners, Christ died for us.

⁹ Much more then, being now justified by his blood,
we shall be saved from wrath through him.

¹⁰ For if, when we were enemies, we were reconciled to God by the death of his Son, much more, being reconciled, we shall be saved by his life.

God gave proof of His love for us when we were without strength, when we were ungodly, when we were sinners, and when we were enemies. The giving of the life of Jesus Christ is the proof of His love. The death of Jesus Christ reconciled us to God. Jesus Christ is a complete savior! Jesus Christ paid the price required for the redemption of mankind. He was the perfect substitute and sacrifice for your sins.

Eternal life is now available because of his death, resurrection, ascension, and the giving of the gift of holy spirit on the day of Pentecost. We can receive the spirit of God. The spirit of God is our completeness in Christ.

Colossians 1:12, 13

¹² Giving thanks unto the Father, which hath made us meet [adequate] to be partakers of the inheritance of the saints in light:

¹³ Who hath delivered us from the power of darkness, and hath translated *us* into the kingdom of his dear Son:

We are partakers of the inheritance of the saints in light. Have you ever received an earthly inheritance? If you have, I am sure it was rather exciting. It may have thrilled your heart. It may have been very valuable in the material realm. Well, you have received an inheritance from God! God has made you adequate to be a partaker of His inheritance.

You also have been delivered, or rescued, from the exercised power of darkness. God has given you citizenship in His kingdom. Is there any reason to feel as if you do not belong? Why would you ever think that you were inadequate? You are adequate! Not in yourself, but in what God has done for you through Christ.

Romans 8:1

There is therefore now no condemnation to them which are in Christ Jesus, who walk not after the flesh, but after the Spirit.

Part of your completeness in Christ is that there is no condemnation from God. When God looks at you, He sees a righteous, sanctified, redeemed son – because you are complete in Christ! You show forth this completeness in your day-by-day living when you are thinking the Word and acting on the Word. There never, ever, ever is any condemnation from God toward you! You should never condemn yourself! You are to see yourself as your Heavenly Father sees you, putting on the mind of Christ.

Ephesians 1:2

Grace *be* to you, and peace, from God our Father, and *from* the Lord Jesus Christ.

You have received grace from God. Grace is undeserved, divine favor from God to you. You have received grace from God, and not only grace, but peace. Peace is the absence of all strife, all fighting. You are at peace with God. You have received peace from your Heavenly Father. God is not fighting with you. He is not waiting for you to make a mistake, so He can beat you over the head. God has given you peace. Peace is yours in this most tumultuous world.

Ephesians 1:3

Blessed *be* the God and Father of our Lord Jesus Christ, who hath blessed us with all spiritual blessings in heavenly *places* in Christ:

We have received all spiritual blessings. These spiritual blessings are in the heavenlies in Christ. If you have all spiritual blessings, are you lacking blessings? No. God has done a complete and perfect work, and He has blessed you with all spiritual blessings. The *all spiritual blessings* are part of what make up your completeness in Christ.

Ephesians 2:4

But God, who is rich in mercy, for his great love wherewith he loved us,

God is abounding in His mercy toward us because of His rich love. Mercy is the withholding of earned judgment. The judgment is withheld because we, as sons of God, have already been judged in Christ. We are now found to be righteous and complete in Christ. This mercy is the love of God extended to us when we least deserved it.

Ephesians 2:5-9

⁵ Even when we were dead in sins, hath quickened us together with Christ, (by grace ye are saved;)

⁶ And hath raised us up together, and made us sit together in heavenly places in Christ Jesus:

⁷ That in the ages to come he might shew the exceeding riches of his grace in his kindness toward us through Christ Jesus.

⁸ For by grace are ye saved through faith; and that not of yourselves: it is the gift of God:

⁹ Not of works, lest any man should boast.

You are saved by God's grace. Salvation is not of your own works. How many people have you met who thought they were saved because they went to the right church, or faithfully attended Sunday school, or never drank an ounce of liquor, or never smoked a cigarette? Well, none of those will save anyone. We are saved by God's grace and the perfect, complete work of His only begotten son Jesus Christ.

If my salvation was of my works, and I did a better work than you, then I could say I had a greater salvation. If you did a better work than me, then you could say your salvation was greater. God's Word says it is by God's grace that we are saved, and that salvation is not of works lest any man should boast!

We all came from the same boat. Ephesians 2:1 and 12 say that "we were all dead in trespasses and sins" and "were without God and had no hope." Dead men cannot do good works. Men and women without God have no hope. There is no spiritual life for a man or woman until he or she accepts God's solution to the sin problem: the Lord Jesus Christ.

None of us can save ourselves by our own works. We are saved by God's grace and the complete and perfect work of His only begotten Son Jesus Christ.

When it comes to salvation, works are not the issue. Men and women are dead because of the sin nature. The sin nature has been passed down from generation to generation because of Adam's disobedience. The sin nature is in the blood of all mankind. Jesus Christ had a perfect, sinless blood. He shed his spotless blood for all mankind. His shed blood is the sacrifice that God required for the redemption of mankind. It states in Hebrews 9:22 that "without the shedding of blood there is no remission."

So you see, that no matter how *good* a man or woman might be, if they don't have Christ, they don't have life. They are dead in trespasses and sins – without God and without hope. The state of the very nature of mankind requires men and women to receive God's solution to the problem. The solution: the Lord Jesus Christ!

II Corinthians 5:21

For he [God] hath made him [Jesus] *to be* sin for us, who knew [by experience] no sin; that we might be made the righteousness of God in him.

God made Jesus Christ to be sin in place of us. Jesus Christ did not know sin by experience because he was a perfect man. Jesus always did his Father's will. Jesus Christ became sin for us so that we could be made the righteousness of God. How righteous is God? He is as righteous as righteous can be! That is how righteous you are! Do you want to argue with God's Word and say, "That just cannot be," or do you want to accept what God has freely given you by His great grace and mercy? God says you are righteous! Is it because of your good works? No. It is by the complete and perfect work of Jesus Christ.

Hebrews 10:10-14

[10] By the which will we are sanctified through the offering of the body of Jesus Christ once for all.

[11] And every priest standeth daily ministering and offering oftentimes the same sacrifices, which can never take away sins:

[12] But this man, after he had offered one sacrifice for sins for ever, sat down on the right hand of God;

[13] From henceforth expecting till his enemies be made his footstool.

[14] For by one offering he hath perfected for ever them that are sanctified.

Jesus Christ offered to God the one perfect, complete sacrifice for the sin nature and sins of mankind. That one offering of his life has perfected, or completed forever, them that are sanctified.

Do you think that you could improve upon that perfection by your good works? To consider the question is foolish. You are complete in Christ. The right thing to do is to accept and believe what God says He has done for us through Jesus Christ.

The next logical step is to show forth this completeness in Christ in our day-by-day life. How are we to live the completeness that we have in Christ? We demonstrate our completeness by operating the gift of holy spirit. The gift of holy spirit has nine manifestations, which are listed in I Corinthians 12.

Many times, well-intentioned people refer to these manifestations as gifts of the holy spirit. There is only one gift of holy spirit. The gift is the new birth. There are nine evidence, or manifestations, of that spirit. People become born from above by believing in their heart that God raised Jesus Christ from the dead and by confessing with their mouth Jesus as Lord. Then they receive the gift of holy spirit. With the gift is the potential to operate the nine manifestations of holy spirit. The nine manifestations of holy spirit are listed in I Corinthians chapter 12.

I Corinthians 12:7-11

[7] But the manifestation of the Spirit is given to every man to profit withal.

[8] For to one is given by the Spirit the word of wisdom; to another the word of knowledge by the same Spirit;

[9] To another faith [believing] by the same Spirit; to another the gifts of healing by the same Spirit;

[10] To another the working of miracles; to another prophecy; to another discerning of spirits; to another divers kinds of tongues; to another the interpretation of tongues:

[11] But all these worketh that one and the selfsame Spirit, dividing to every man severally [his own] as he [the man] will.

When we operate these manifestations of holy spirit, we begin to show forth the completeness that we have in Christ. These manifestations of holy spirit are available for every born-again believer to operate. They are not for just a chosen few, for God is no respecter of persons. These nine manifestations are the evidence of holy spirit within an individual.

To take it a step further, the operation of these manifestations of holy spirit in your life results in the fruit of the spirit.

Galatians 5:22, 23

[22] But the fruit of the Spirit [NOT the fruit of good works] is love, joy, peace, longsuffering, gentleness, goodness, faith,

[23] Meekness, temperance: against such there is no law.

Fruit results from the operation of the manifestations of the spirit. The fruit is the outcome in the life of an individual who operates their completeness in Christ by way of the manifestations.

How absolutely wonderful it is that our Heavenly Father has given us His gift of holy spirit, and that we have the privilege to operate the manifestations of that gift. Our operation of the gift shows forth the fruit of the spirit in our lives.

These manifestations and fruit show forth some of our completeness in Christ. However, the fullness and greatness of being complete in him will only be known when we see him face-to-face.

Colossians 3:1-4

[1] If [Since] ye then be risen with Christ, seek those things which are above, where Christ sits on the right hand of God.

[2] Set your affection [your thoughts] on things above, not on things on the earth.

[3] For ye are dead, and your life is hid with Christ in God.

[4] When Christ, *who is* our life, shall appear, then shall ye also appear with him in glory.

When *we appear with him in glory* then we shall fully appreciate that we are completely, completely, absolutely complete in him. How exciting it is to know that we are God's children. The Creator of the heavens and earth is your Father. You are complete in Christ! You lack nothing! Today, accept from your Father what has already been accomplished. You are complete in Christ!

Discussion Questions

1. Jesus Christ gave his life for you. What have you received because of his sacrifice?

2. Are you declared righteous by your works or by the work of Jesus Christ? Explain your answer.

3. Can every person who is born-again operate the nine manifestations of holy spirit? Explain your answer.

4. What are the fruit of the spirit as listed in Galatians chapter five?

5. Your life is hid with Christ in God. How do you find that life?

CHAPTER 12

Freedom

This Independence Day weekend, we are commemorating the signing of the Declaration of Independence on July 4, 1776. In God's Word, we see that we have received spiritual freedom in Christ.

John 8:28-32, 36

28 Then said Jesus unto them, When ye have lifted up the Son of man [on the cross], then shall ye know that I am he, and that I do nothing of myself [nothing of my own authority]; but as my Father hath taught me, I speak these things.

29 And he that sent me is with me: the Father hath not left me alone; for I do always those things that please him.

Jesus Christ was not on his own. His Heavenly Father was with him. He spoke and did what his Father directed him to speak and do.

30 As he spake these words, many believed on him.

God knew the hearts of those listening to Jesus. Some were tender and hungry to know God and their Messiah. God always gave Jesus the exact right words to speak to the people present.

> [31] Then said Jesus to those Jews which believed on him, If ye continue in my word [dwell and abide in his Word to the end of believing and living], then are ye my disciples [followers, disciplined ones] indeed;

> [32] And ye shall know the truth, and the truth shall make you free.

In John chapter 17 Jesus Christ stated, "God's Word is Truth."

> [36] If the Son therefore shall make you free, ye shall be free indeed.

You can never be free until you know Jesus Christ as your Lord and Savior. He is the one who has made us free. What is the great freedom that Christ makes available? It is freedom from the bondage of sin!

The sin nature, and the fruit of that nature, is bondage and hold all people captive until they come to Christ.

Today we find our true freedom in Christ, in our acceptance of his substitution for us in his death, and in our identification with him in his resurrection, ascension and his seating at God's right hand.

Jesus Christ became one with us in death so that we might become one with him in life.

Romans 6:1

What shall we say then? Shall we continue [abide or stay in] in sin, that grace may abound?

Looking at the close of the previous chapter, Romans 5:20 and 21 state, "that where sin abounded, grace did much more abound" and "that sin reigned through death and that grace would reign through righteousness."

There are some that say you should not teach too much grace, because then you will give people a license to sin. What is too much grace? God gives His grace so that we might live and have eternal life. God's grace through Jesus Christ covers all sin. All sin in the past, all sin today and all sin tomorrow. There is no shortage of God's grace.

Only a fool would continue in sin so that grace might abound. The eternal life through Christ would not be lost because of the sin, but there would be a lose of eternal rewards. Eternity is a long, long time. Think of the rewards available for those that continue in grace. Now, think of the rewards lost for those that continue in sin. Continuing in God's grace is where the believer reigns in life.

Romans 6:2

God forbid. How shall we, that are dead to sin, live any longer therein?

"God forbid" is an expression of extreme horror. Do not even let it be thought of! The very thought of continuing in sin that grace may abound is revolting.

When our identity is in Christ, it is impossible to continue in sin since we are dead to sin.

Remember II Corinthians 5:21, "For he hath made him to be sin for us, who knew no sin; that we might be made the righteousness of God in him."

Jesus Christ literally received what we deserved – death. We received what he deserved – life.

Romans 6:3

Know ye not, that so many of us as were baptized into Jesus Christ were baptized into his death?

"Baptized into his death" is not referring to water baptism. It is our full immersion into his death in our identification with him. We are immersed in Christ Jesus. We are fully identified with him in his death on the cross. In all that he accomplished - when he proclaimed, "it is finished" – we died with him on the cross. Jesus Christ poured out his life all the way to death. In the sight of God, we were with Jesus on the cross. He is our substitute in taking the penalty for sin – death.

Romans 6:4

Therefore we are buried with him by baptism into death: that like as Christ was raised up from the dead by the glory of the Father, even so we also should walk in newness of life.

In our identification with Christ, we were buried with him. He was in the grave for three days and three nights. From God's perspective, we were buried with him!

Then Christ was raised from the dead by the glory of the Father! Jesus is the only one who has been raised from the dead and is alive today. There is not one other person in all the history of mankind that died for you and then was raised from the dead by God.

When Jesus Christ was raised from the dead, he received a NEW life!

We also are to live that NEW life! It is NEW in quality. It is a life free of sin, sickness, and fear. It is a life of joy above the circumstances of life. It is a life of trust in God as your Heavenly Father. It is a relationship of full sharing with your Father God.

It is the life of John 14:12, "to do the same works as Jesus Christ and even greater works!"

Romans 6:5

For if we have been planted together in the likeness of his death, we shall be also in the likeness of his resurrection:

What is the likeness of his resurrected body? It is a body free of sin and sickness. It is an incorruptible body. It is a body powered by holy spirit - unlimited in scope and ability. It is a glorified body! At his magnificent RETURN we shall have the same! What a HOPE! Hold the Word of truth in your heart to the end, that you live your life today in light of his sure RETURN for you.

Romans 6:6

Knowing this, that our old man is [was] crucified with him, that the body of sin might be destroyed [made ineffective or paralyzed], that henceforth we should not serve sin.

The old nature handed down to all mankind through Adam, and all that proceeds from that nature, was crucified with Jesus Christ on the cross. Why would anyone ever choose to live in sin, sickness, and fear when it was crucified with Christ?

The old nature is NOW paralyzed! It is paralyzed! It has no power over you. You no longer need to serve or be obedient to that evil and corrupt nature. The only thing the old nature gives is death.

Hold the Word of truth in your heart to the end, that you live your life today in light of his RETURN for you.

The resurrection of the Lord Jesus Christ has given life! Who does not want life? Many complain about the life they live; it can only be because they do not know of the life available in Christ! Those that know and still complain, they need to put on the mind of Christ and walk in newness of life!

Romans 6:7-9

⁷ For he that is dead is freed from sin.

You are dead because you died with Christ. You are now free from the sin nature.

> ⁸ Now if we be dead with Christ, we believe that we shall also live with him:
>
> ⁹ Knowing that Christ being raised from the dead dieth no more; death hath no more dominion over him.

Death has no more dominion over Christ Jesus because he has been raised from the dead. Today he is seated at God's right hand in the heavens.

Literally, for those that are born again of God's spirit, death no longer has dominion. You have the spirit of Christ within!

What is it that keeps men and women from walking in the newness of life made available in the new birth? Fear.

Fear of what others may think. Fear of failing. Fear that God will not be true to the promises in His Word. Fear is the most foul and evil four-letter word in all vocabulary.

Hebrews 2:14, 15

¹⁴ Forasmuch then as the children are partakers of flesh and blood, he also himself likewise took part of the same; that through death he might destroy [paralyze or make ineffective] him that had the power of death, that is, the devil;

¹⁵ And deliver [or set free] them who through fear of death were all their lifetime subject to bondage.

The fear of death is the root fear of all fears. Fear places people in bondage.

Death was defeated in Christ. Jesus has been raised from the dead! The fear of death has no more dominion, or power, over you because you are as Christ. In your identification with Christ, you have all that he has.

You may physically die before the Lord returns, but when he returns you will be raised from the dead to live through all eternity!

The Christian church, for the most part, has lived so far below par because of fear. Today is the day to eliminate the fear in your life and recognize who you are in Christ. Live the life that God has given you!

Romans 6:10

For in that he died, he died unto sin once: but in that he liveth, he liveth unto God.

Jesus Christ died unto sin once. He now lives unto God forever. God raised him from the dead.

Hebrews 10:12-14

¹² But this man [Jesus Christ], after he had offered *one* sacrifice for sins *for ever*, sat down on the right hand of God;

[13] From henceforth expecting till his enemies be made his footstool.

[14] For by one offering [his life] he hath perfected [made to be complete] for ever them [you] that are sanctified [set apart].

Romans 6:11

Likewise reckon ye also yourselves to be dead indeed unto sin, but alive unto God through Jesus Christ our Lord.

Likewise – since you died with him, you were buried with him, you were raised with him, and you have ascended with him — RECKON.

To "reckon" is to logically conclude that you are *permanently dead* unto sin and *permanently alive* unto God.

In your identification with your Lord, you have great freedom. You now have freedom from the bondage of sin and freedom from fear. No matter what circumstance you might find yourself in, your freedom in Christ transcends all situations.

As you renew your mind to what your Heavenly Father has made you to be by putting on the mind of Christ, you will show to the world what true freedom is.

Jesus Christ's death was not in vain. He saw your value as he hung on the tree. He saw the impact your life would have today in this world as you stood boldly upon the truth of God's Word.

Today, this world so desperately needs men and women to live the love of God, with the Word of God burning in their hearts to the end they cannot help but speak those things which they have seen and heard.

God's Word is truth! God really has made Himself known to you today. It is time to take God at His Word! Decide right now that today is a new day. The past is past. Tomorrow is not guaranteed. Today is the day to believe that you are who God's Word says you are. Now is the time to live in the spiritual freedom within which you have been called.

Our rallying cry ought to be, "Obey God rather than men." The eternal rewards from God far outweigh the fleeting rewards of this world.

Let God be glorified in your life. Let it be said today by those that see your life, "What power and authority God has given unto men!"

Discussion Questions

1. True freedom is found in Christ. What is the freedom that Christ makes available?

2. Is it possible to receive too much grace? Explain.

3. Fear is what keeps people from living the life God has called them too. Is there any fear holding you back from living for God? What can you do to eliminate fear?

4. Obedience to your Heavenly Father will result in great blessing to you. Relate a time when you were obedient to God's direction and the result of that obedience.

5. Remember a time when God delivered you from a fear or bad circumstance.

CHAPTER 13

Speak God's Word

In this so-called enlightened day and time is the preaching of God's Word profitable? Is it a worthwhile endeavor for you or me to speak to others of Jesus Christ and all that he has accomplished?

Let's answer those questions.

I Corinthians 1:17-18

[17] For Christ sent me not to baptize, but to preach the gospel: not with wisdom of words, lest the cross of Christ [what the cross accomplished] should be made of none effect.

[18] For the preaching of the cross [the preaching of Jesus and his accomplished work] is to them that perish foolishness [or nonsense]; but unto us which are saved it is the power of God.

God sent Paul to preach the gospel of Jesus Christ. Paul was not sent to preach a "feel good, you can go your own way, do whatever you like it's all good" kind of message He did not use the wisdom of words to try to trick or coerce. He spoke the good news of Jesus Christ!

If you are reading this and you think the preaching of Jesus is utter nonsense and foolishness and that only someone weak would trust in Jesus, well I would be concerned, because that is how one that is perishing thinks!

The preaching of the cross is foolishness to them that perish. But to those which are saved, it is the power of God!

The preaching of the cross is salvation to those who believe!

The preaching of the cross is comfort to those who are afflicted!

The preaching of the cross is health to those who are sick!

The preaching of the cross is peace to those who are tormented!

The preaching of the cross is strength to those who are weak!

I Corinthians 1:20

Where is the wise? [one wise in the things of this world] where is the scribe? [one skilled in philosophy or the man-made religions of this world] where is the disputer of this world? [one who inquires and debates the things of this age] hath not God made foolish the wisdom of this world?

What are some examples of this world's wisdom?

- There is no God.

- Jesus was a good man, but he was not the son of God nor did he die for my sins.

- I do not need Jesus. I am a good person.

- Everyone goes to heaven and is a child of God.

- The government will take care of me. You know they are working on melding humans and machines and then we will all live forever.

- We all have a little god in us, and we need to just tap into the universal consciousness.

- Just be tolerant of each other. We all believe in the same god anyway.

That is the wisdom of this world!

I Corinthians 1:21-25

[21] For after that in the wisdom of God the world by [man's] wisdom knew not God, it pleased God by the foolishness of preaching to save them that believe.

[22] For the Jews require a sign [show me a sign brother then I'll believe], and the Greeks [Gentiles – all others] seek after [worldly] wisdom [intellectual comfort]:

[23] But we preach Christ crucified, unto the Jews a stumblingblock, and unto the Greeks foolishness;

²⁴ But unto them which are called, both Jews and Greeks, Christ the power of God, and the wisdom of God.

To those that believe, Christ is the power of God and the wisdom of God. He is the power of God because God raised him from the dead. He is the wisdom of God because he is God's solution to the dire dilemma mankind found itself in after the fall of Adam.

²⁵ Because the foolishness of God is wiser than men; and the weakness of God is stronger than men.

If God could be foolish, His foolishness is still wiser than the wisest of men. If God could be weak, His weakness would still be stronger than the strongest of men.

I Corinthians 2:1-8

¹ And I, brethren, when I came to you, came not with excellency of speech [lofty words] or of wisdom, declaring unto you the testimony [or mystery] of God.

² For I determined not to know any thing among you, save Jesus Christ, and him crucified.

³ And I was with you in weakness, and in fear, and in much trembling.

Verse three should be translated, "I was with you in reverence and obedience," as a servant is obedient to his master. Who was Paul's master? God the Father and the Lord Jesus Christ. Remember, we read in chapter one that Christ sent Paul to preach the gospel.

[4] And my speech and my preaching was not with enticing words of man's wisdom [clever words], but in demonstration of the Spirit and of power:

Paul operated the spirit of God. There were signs, miracles and wonders wherever and whenever Paul preached the gospel.

[5] That your faith [believing] should not stand in the wisdom of men, but in the power of God.

[6] Howbeit we speak wisdom among them that are perfect [mature]: yet not the wisdom of this world, nor of the princes of this world, that come to nought:

I Corinthians 2:6 (Phillips translation)

We do, of course, speak "wisdom" among those who are spiritually mature, but it is not what is called wisdom by this world, nor by the powers-that-be, who soon will be only the powers that have been.

Who are the powers that be? The god of this world – the devil and his minions. They soon will be only the powers that have been!

[7] But we speak the wisdom of God in a mystery [regarding the mystery], even the hidden wisdom [hidden since the foundation of the world until God made it known to the Apostle Paul], which God ordained before the world unto our glory:

Unto whose glory? Our glory!

⁸ Which none of the princes of this world knew: for
had they known it, they would not have crucified the
Lord of glory.

None of the princes of this world knew the mystery that was
hidden in God, the mystery being that both Judean and all the
nations of the world could be of one body through Christ,
and the riches of the mystery being Christ in you, the hope of
glory! The devil and his spirits did not know the mystery, nor
the riches of the glory of the mystery. Had they known the
mystery and its riches; they never would have crucified the
Lord Jesus Christ.

Jesus Christ would still be alive today had they not crucified
him. How many places could Jesus Christ be when he was
here upon earth? Only one.
How many places can he be
today? He can be everywhere
there is a born-again son of
God because of the Christ
within! The church today has
tremendous authority and
power! The church can do the
same works as Jesus Christ did and even greater. (See John
14:12)

It is Christ in you,
the hope of glory!

I Corinthians 3:1-4

¹ And I, brethren, could not speak unto you as unto
spiritual, but as unto carnal, even as unto babes in
Christ.

[2] I have fed you with milk, and not with meat: for hitherto ye were not able to bear it, neither yet now are ye able.

Why?

[3] For ye are yet carnal: for whereas there is among you envying, and strife, and divisions, are ye not carnal, and walk as men?

[4] For while one saith, I am of Paul; and another, I am of Apollos; are ye not carnal?

Don't we see that today? Some say, "I'm with this group," or "I stand with that man." How about we stand with God and His son, the Lord Jesus Christ? God is God, and Christ Jesus is the head of the body. All members of the body of Christ have the same head. Not any one member is any more important or any more valuable than another. Each member is in the body where it pleases God! Carnal thinking, which issues in envy, strife and division, is the wisdom of man. It is worldly wisdom, and it is foolish.

I Corinthians 3:5-9

[5] Who then is Paul, and who is Apollos, but ministers by whom ye believed, even as the Lord gave to every man?

[6] I have planted, Apollos watered; but God gave the increase.

[7] So then neither is he that planteth any thing, neither he that watereth; but God that giveth the increase.

[8] Now he that planteth and he that watereth are one: and every man shall receive his own reward according to his own labour.

[9] For we are labourers together with God:

In the fall of 1974, my college roommate's mom said to me, "Don't stop reading the Word." At the time, I had no idea what she was talking about. Later, I came to know that the Word she was talking about was the Bible.

In the fall of 1976, I went to a Chicago Bears game at Soldier Field in Chicago with some college friends. Outside of the stadium, there were several people handing out Bible tracts and talking about God and Jesus Christ. I remember talking with a couple of them, and my heart burned within to know more of what they knew about God.

The conversation was short, as I was hurried along by some of my friends. The seed of God's Word that was planted that day landed in good soil and it has produced fruit over the years.

In May of 1977, the Gideons were on my college campus handing out New Testament Bibles. That morning, I received my first Bible. I had never read the Bible before, as I was raised in a Christian denomination that did not encourage Bible reading.

Shortly thereafter on a Tuesday evening, I returned home lonely and discouraged. I picked up that Bible and began to read words that changed my life forever. I could not put it down. That night I was born again as I read Romans 10:9 and

10. On the inside back cover of the pocket-size New Testament, I remember signing my name and entering the date on the fill-in blanks to indicate that I had confessed Jesus as my Lord.

After becoming a son of God, I began to visit several churches throughout the area. I needed to find someone that could teach me the Word of God. I was hungry to know the truth.

It was in the spring of 1978 when I attended a small Bible fellowship in one of the dorms where I began to gain an understanding of the scriptures. I was taught God's love both in word and deed. I will always be thankful for those that took the time to work with me and to help me in my walk with God. I know there is a great eternal reward for each of them.

Did any of those first three encounters fail because I did not go to church with them? No! All were a success because they planted and watered the seed of God's Word in my heart.

Now, back to our original question.

In this so called "enlightened day and time," is the preaching of God's Word profitable?

Is it a worthwhile endeavor for you to speak to others of Jesus Christ and all that he has accomplished?

I would say, "yes and amen!"

In Acts 5:20, the angel instructed the apostles to "go, stand and speak in the temple to the people all the words of this life."

Let us go, stand, and speak on the streets, in the malls, door-to-door, at the market, at the beach, at work, when on vacation, to the people, all the words of this life! Let it be said of us that we have filled our cities with the doctrine of Jesus Christ, and that we have shown forth the wisdom and power of God! Never let anyone hinder you or discourage you from speaking God's Word.

Our labor is not in vain. There are great rewards throughout all eternity for those that plant and water the hearts of men and women with the Word of God.

Even so, come quickly Lord Jesus!

Discussion Questions

1. Are you sent to preach the gospel of Jesus Christ? How might you be most effective in preaching the gospel?

2. What are some examples of Godly wisdom that you would like to demonstrate in your life?

3. What are some examples of worldly wisdom you know to avoid?

4. Think back to a time when someone spoke God's Word to you. What type of impact did that have on your life?

5. What does it mean that Paul and Apollos planted and watered, and God gave the increase?

CHAPTER 14

Are We Living in The End Times?

Today, the Christian church, for the most part, has lost the immense joy in anticipation of looking to the hope of our Lord's return. Some have us living in the book of Revelation today, where the wrath of God is poured out upon those that have rejected God. Others are not even aware the Lord is returning and hold onto the belief that when one dies, they immediately enter the presence of the Lord.

The truth regarding the end times and the events surrounding that period is made known in God's Word.

Let's begin in Ephesians 1:10.

Ephesians 1:10

That in the dispensation [administration] of the fulness of times he [God] might gather together in one all things in Christ, both which are in heaven, and which are on earth; even in him:

God's timetable is found in the administration of the fullness of times. That is the moment the Lord Jesus Christ will return. The Amplified Bible translates the "fullness of times" as the climax of the ages. At the climax of the ages, God calls His children to meet the Lord in the air. When the Lord Jesus Christ returns to gather the church, we will meet him in the clouds. We will be lifted off the earth in our new body to meet him in the air! What a glorious time of rejoicing! What a wonderful inheritance!

Chapter two of II Thessalonians will give us a clearer understanding of the Lord's return.

II Thessalonians 2:1-3

¹Now we beseech you, brethren, by the coming of our Lord Jesus Christ, and by our gathering together unto him,

²That ye be not soon shaken in mind, or be troubled, neither by spirit, nor by word, nor by letter as from us, as that the day of Christ is at hand.

³Let no man deceive you by any means: for that day shall not come, except there come a falling away first, and that man of sin be revealed, the son of perdition;

In verse one, "the coming of our Lord Jesus Christ" is his personal presence. This is the moment that we see him face to face! It is the instant when the dead in Christ are raised and we who are living are changed to meet him in the air. The dead put on incorruption, and those which are alive put on immortality!

It is this great hope of the Lord's return that gives us the patience to endure the tribulations and pressures of this life. The Thessalonian church needed reassurance of the Lord's return. We do too! The assurance of the Lord's return is part of the reason this great epistle of II Thessalonians was written.

Let's read verse two again.

> ² That ye be not soon shaken in mind, or be troubled, neither by spirit, nor by word, nor by letter as from us, as that the day of Christ is at hand.

Do not be frightened from any source – by spirit, by word, nor by letter – that the day of the Lord has set in or begun.

The Thessalonian church was a tremendous example of speaking and living God's Word. They were also under extreme pressure and persecution to give up and not to stand for the one true God. In this epistle, Paul lovingly beseeched them by the return of Jesus Christ. In other words, "It's all worth it!" Walk in love and boldly speak and stand for the truth! Do not be frightened by what anyone may say regarding the day of the Lord that it has already happened!

Walk in love and boldly speak and stand for the truth!

What is the day of the Lord? The day of the Lord is the judgment of God as detailed throughout the book of

Revelation. The Thessalonian believers are told not to be frightened or troubled that the day of the Lord has begun!

The church of the body of Christ, to which you belong, will never face the judgment of God as detailed throughout the book of Revelation. We have been judged in the life, death, and resurrection of Jesus Christ! If we have not been judged in Jesus Christ, then he died in vain. He wasted his life.

How often today we hear preachers, ministers and writers proclaim that we are living at the time of God's judgment – the Book of Revelation! That is exactly what the Thessalonian believers were told by some, and they became afraid that it was true. Many of God's people today are fearful that they must endure the wrath of God, which God will show upon an unrepentant world. There is no comfort in that!

In I Thessalonians chapter four where the return of Jesus Christ is detailed, we are told to comfort one another with the words regarding his return. There is wonderful comfort, peace, and rest in knowing God loves you. Before the great judgment of the ages, you will be gathered together with Christ to be seated in heavenly places.

Do not confuse the judgment of God in the book of Revelation with persecution. The Thessalonian believers were persecuted by the unbelievers in the first-century church. Today, God's people are persecuted by an unbelieving world. The persecution that comes from unbelievers IS NOT the pouring out of God's wrath! God the Father loves His children! God would never in a million years utilize the devil and the devil's minions to bring hardship upon those whom

He has redeemed through Jesus Christ! To consider that He would, indicates a lack of understanding of how loving and graciously kind our Heavenly Father is!

How can we know that the day of the Lord has not yet begun?

Right here in the context, the very next verse.

II Thessalonians 2:3

³ Let no man deceive you by any means: *for that day* [what day? The day of the Lord] *shall not come*, except there come a falling away first, and that man of sin be revealed, the son of perdition;

The key in understanding this verse is the phrase "except there come a falling away first." The King James translation, and many modern translations as well as commentaries, have handled these words to infer that there will be a departure of Christians from believing God's Word. Alternatively, they might call it *apostasy*, or a departure from the faith.

In the Greek, it literally means *a separation away from* or *a departure from.*

The modern interpretation has implied that it was God's people departing from God. That is not so!

It is the departing of God's people from this world at the time of the gathering together when the Lord Jesus Christ returns. It is when we meet him in the air, as detailed in chapter four of I Thessalonians and in I Corinthians chapter 15.

It is also translated properly as *a departure* in the Geneva Bible, the Cranmer Bible, and the Tyndale Bible.

> ³ Let no man deceive you by any means: *for that day* [what day? The day of the Lord – the judgments of God in the book of Revelation] *shall not come*, except there come a falling away first [a departure of God's saints from the earth at the time of the return of Jesus Christ], and that man of sin be revealed, the son of perdition;

Another key to the understanding of this verse is in considering the phrase "that man of sin be revealed, the son of perdition."

The man of sin and lawlessness, the man of perdition, is the antichrist. The antichrist will be a man who is literally controlled by the devil. That man of lawlessness will rule the world with an evil heart, as detailed in the Word of God.

He has not yet stepped into his position of rebellion. The day of the Lord, the book of Revelation, does not begin until there is a departure of God's saints from the earth at the return of Jesus Christ, and then, THEN the man of lawlessness will be revealed.

Knowing that "the man of lawlessness" has not yet been revealed and is not yet ruling this world, indicates that we are NOT living in the book of Revelation and the righteous judgments of our God!

Let no one deceive you by any means, by any communication, that we are living in the days of the judgment of God as written in Revelation!

II Thessalonians 2:4-7

> [4] Who [the antichrist] opposeth and exalteth himself above all that is called God, or that is worshipped; so that he as God sitteth in the temple of God, shewing himself that he is God.

The great counterfeit, the Antichrist, will endeavor to show himself as the one true God.

> [5] Remember ye not, that, when I was yet with you, I told you these things?

> [6] And now ye know what withholdeth that he might be revealed in his time.

> [7] For the mystery of iniquity doth already work: only he who now letteth will let, until he be taken out of the way.

It is not yet the antichrist's time. The antichrist has not yet been revealed. There are those against Christ, iniquity is working in this world, but THE Antichrist has not yet been revealed. And if someone tells you they know who the Antichrist is, they are guessing. He has not yet been revealed.

There is something withholding the devil from manifesting himself through THE Antichrist.

In verse seven, the word "letteth" would be better translated to hold or restrain.

Who is withholding? Who is restraining? Who is not allowing the Antichrist of the book of Revelation to make himself known and rule the world?

Verse seven says, "until he be taken out of the way." It is God's children who have the spirit of the one true God that hold back the adversary, the devil, from the fulfillment of his lawlessness and destruction through THE Antichrist.

It all ties together; the day of the Lord, the judgments of God, the revealing of the Antichrist CANNOT commence until after the church of the body of Christ has been gathered together with the Lord Jesus Christ!

The exact moment of Christ's return is unknown by men, BUT it is absolute!

II Thessalonians 2:8-12

[8] And then [after the church is removed] shall that Wicked be revealed, whom the Lord shall consume with the spirit of his mouth, and shall destroy with the brightness of his coming:

[9] Even him, whose coming is after the working of Satan with all power and signs and lying wonders,

[10] And with all deceivableness of unrighteousness in them that perish; because they received not the love of the truth, that they might be saved.

Some people choose not to believe. God desires that all men be saved and come to a knowledge of the truth. Some just do not want to believe and they are the ones that are perishing.

> [11] And for this cause God shall send them strong delusion, that they should believe a lie:

> [12] That they all might be damned who believed not the truth, but had pleasure in unrighteousness [or well pleased with unrighteousness].

Many people today take pleasure in unrighteousness. They call good "evil" and they call evil "good." They make laws and rules that call darkness "light" and light they call "darkness." It is all around, and the world will continue to deteriorate until the return of the Lord Jesus Christ.

The lights of the world need to shine like never before. How do we shine? We shine by living love. How do we live love? It is not a sweet syrupy love; it is a love that is unafraid to speak the truth of God's Word to a corrupt and dying world. Now is the time for you, a called saint of God, to be and live God's Word.

He is returning and at that great and notable moment of his appearing, there will be great rejoicing by the saints of God. There will also be great wailing and gnashing of teeth by those that have rejected the truth.

II Thessalonians 2:13-17

[13] But we are bound to give thanks alway to God for you, brethren beloved of the Lord, because God hath from the beginning chosen you to salvation through sanctification of the Spirit and belief of the truth:

[14] Whereunto he called you by our gospel, to the obtaining of the glory of our Lord Jesus Christ.

[15] Therefore, brethren, stand fast, and hold the traditions which ye have been taught, whether by word, or our epistle.

[16] Now our Lord Jesus Christ himself, and God, even our Father, which hath loved us, and hath given us everlasting consolation and good hope through grace,

[17] Comfort your hearts, and stablish you in every good word and work.

What a comfort to know that we will NOT go through the righteous judgment of God as detailed throughout the book of Revelation. Do not be deceived by those that teach otherwise. There are many false prophets in the world today, even as the spirit of antichrist is at work.

What a comfort to know our Lord will absolutely return, gathering us together unto him.

What a comfort to know that eternal rewards await each of us. It will take all eternity for you to enjoy all that your Father has in store for you.

II Corinthians 5:10

For we must all appear before the judgment [bema] seat of Christ; that every one may receive the things done in his body, according to that he hath done, whether it be good or bad.

The word "judgment" in the Greek is the word *bema*.

The *bema* in the Greek culture, and Biblically, is a place where rewards are handed out. Your faithfulness to believe God will result in rewards and crowns, as detailed in other parts of scripture.

Today is a day like no other. The Lord could return at any moment and then the end times, as spoken of in Revelation, will begin. It is our joy and privilege until that instant to love an unloving world, as God loves, and to speak His Word making salvation and victory available to all.

Discussion Questions

1. According to Ephesians 1:10, what will happen in the fulness of times?

2. What is the Christian believer's great hope?

3. According to II Thessalonians, what is withholding the devil from making manifest his man, the Antichrist?

4. What possibilities open up for you in this life knowing that you have already been judged in Christ?

5. When you appear at the judgment seat [*bema*] of Christ, what will you receive?

Order Additional Copies

Postal Order Form for:

God's Magnificent Goodness
Volume One: Victorious Christian Living

Mail Orders to: The Solution
PO Box 9002, Naperville, IL 60567

Price: $14.00 + $3.50 shipping and handling (Add $1.00 shipping for each additional book.)

Please Print

Quantity: _____ Total Price: _____

Name: _____

Address: _____

City: _____ State: _____

Zip Code: _____

Phone (optional): _____

Email: _____

Orders may also be placed online.

TheSolutionRadioShow.com

ShopTheSolution.com

Email: info@TheSolutionRadioShow.com